# The Times of the Signs

# The Times of the Signs

*What the Bible really teaches about signs and gifts*

**David Noble**

# Foreword

This book is largely as it was originally written, although my late father's wording has been changed in a few places to improve readability. In addition, I have re-formatted where appropriate, and checked and corrected Scriptural quotes where this was necessary. A third appendix on the purpose of tongues has also been added. The view presented therein is similar though not identical to that presented in my father's book and served as at least part of the stimulus for his own fuller work.

The Bible translation used throughout is that of John Nelson Darby, which is well-known for both its accuracy and literality.

Two abbreviations have been commonly used: OT for Old Testament and NT for New Testament.

All that remains to be said is that this is the first volume (God willing) of several books on subjects of interest to serious Christians.

Steve Noble
July 2023

# Preface

The following pages represent the outcome of a study by the author into the signs of Scripture, particularly those of the New Testament. That God gave signs in the past is indisputable to all who believe the Bible. To such there is also no doubt that God will give signs again in the future. Whether or not signs should be expected today is the question that this booklet seeks to address. The author will leave his readers to answer that question before the Lord after they have read the booklet.

David Noble
2006

# Contents


**1** *Chapter 1:* ***General Introduction***

- The One and Only Test
- Distinction and Identification
- The Identification of the Signs with Israel

**7** *Chapter 2:* ***The Time of the Signs Covered by the Gospels***

- Introduction
- The Object of the Lord's Coming to Israel
- The Identification of the Messiah
- The Gentile Exceptions
- Why were the Signs Miracles?
- The Continuance of the Signs
- Summary

**17** *Chapter 3:* ***The Continuation of the Signs During the Lord's Absence***

- Introduction
- The Bearing of Hebrews 2 on Signs
- The Signs of Mark 16
- Summary

**23** *Chapter 4:* ***The Time for the Peculiar Sign of Tongues***

- Introduction
- The Significance of Tongues
- Tongues in Acts 2
- Tongues in Acts 10
- Tongues in Acts 19
- Summary

**31** *Chapter 5:* ***The Time that the Testimony was Restricted to Jerusalem (Acts 1–7)***

- Introduction
- The Continuance of the Testimony of the Gospels
- God's Final Testimony to Jerusalem
- Summary

**37** *Chapter 6:* ***The Time that the Testimony went Beyond Jerusalem (Acts 8–28)***

- Introduction
- The Advent of the Testimony to the Gentiles
- The Apostolic Nature of the Testimonial Exercise of Signs
- To the Jew First
- The Miracles of Paul
- The Absence of the Mystery in the Book of Acts
- Sects and the Way
- Summary

**49** *Chapter 7:* ***The Mystery and The Cessation of the Signs***

- Introduction
- The Distinction between Signs and Gifts
- The Thirteenth Chapter of 1 Corinthians
- The Mystery
- Summary

**59** *Chapter 8:* ***The Present Time***

- Introduction
- The Gifts in Ephesians
- The Great Deception
- The Miracle Workers of Matthew Seven
- The Will of God
- A Final Word from Deuteronomy
- Summary

**67** *Chapter 9:* ***Summing Up***

- Overall Summary
- Conclusions

**73** *Appendices*

1. The Meaning of the Word *Tongues* in Scripture
2. The Meaning of "when that which is perfect has come" (1 Cor. 13: 10)
3. The Purpose of Tongues

# Chapter 1

# General Introduction

There are many today, largely under the umbrella of the Pentecostal/Charismatic Movement, that claim to speak with tongues, heal the sick, cast out demons, and there are even reports of the dead being raised. In short, they assert miracles. Furthermore, they maintain that they can prophesy, and some say that they have fresh revelations from God. There are even those that assert that they are apostles. This is not new for we read even in the days of the apostles that "thou hast tried them who say that themselves [are] apostles and are not, and hast found them liars" (Rev. 2: 2).

The more extreme among them even state that these 'end–time' apostles and prophets are far greater than Peter and Paul. Some go so far as to exalt their 'ministry' above the Scriptures, thereby making the Bible subservient! Such is the ungodly arrogance of man! Even the milder members of this 'signs–and–wonders' movement contend that as long as the Church is here on earth we will have all the original gifts. In particular, the gift of tongues is often claimed to be the proof that a person has believed the Gospel and been indwelt by the Holy Spirit. While extreme views, such as exalting 'ministry' above the Bible, may justly cause the conversion of its proponents to be questioned, I also recognise that there are many genuine believers in the movement, even though they are sadly deceived concerning signs and gifts.

Now as my reader will at once realise, claims for miracles are easy to make but are harder to substantiate. How should one test such assertions? How does one know whether these miracles come from God? Clearly, if they turn out to be false, their source is not God. Indeed, many of these claims of healing cannot be tested by the average believer and those that could be tested do not seem to occur! I could not tell whether a man who was said to have terminal stomach cancer has now been cured. However, I could tell if an acquaintance who previously had only one leg now had two! This is exactly the thought behind the comment of one wit, who on visiting Lourdes (where the Roman Catholics claim that healings have taken place), said that he saw many redundant wheelchairs there but no wooden legs! The Lord Jesus warned that before His return "there shall arise false

Christs, and false prophets, and shall give great signs and wonders, so as to mislead, if possible, even the elect" (Matt. 24: 24). Notice that the danger stated by the Lord is of genuine believers (the elect) being misled. So, am I to go by what I hear? Should I judge by what my eyes see? Is my discernment so sharp, my perception so focused, that the Devil cannot fool me? The answer is a definite ***no***. Again, should experience interpret Scripture, or should Scripture interpret experience? Those who use experience to interpret the Bible make the Bible subservient to experience and in so doing deny its supreme authority.

**The One and Only Test**

As demons can give signs (see Rev. 16: 14), miraculous signs do not prove divine intervention. Again, in Matt. 7: 21–23 we read of some who claimed to do miraculous works under the Lord's authority but despite that, the Lord called them "workers of lawlessness" (v23). In doing so, He did not challenge their claim to miraculous works, but He did deny that they had carried out the will of God. They did the miracles, but they did not do the Father's will. Miracles and the like neither prove a person to be a believer or that he is doing the will of God. The miracles that the apostles did were "according to his will" (Heb. 2: 4).

The test is not whether today's miracles are genuine or false, it is not even whether the power exercised is demonic or divine, it is ***whether it is God's will that men and women should perform miracles***. How do I determine that? From the Scriptures and nowhere else. Hence, I do not even attempt to check if the claimed miracles are genuine (or the source of the power behind them), but I go to the Bible to see if it is God's will that there should be miracles and signs at the present time. The Bible is not just the final arbiter in the matter—***it is the only arbiter***. Experience is no test. The crux of the matter is not whether these phenomena take place or not, but ***whether it is God's will that they should do so***. Is it the time for signs? The answer lies in the Scriptures: "To the law and the testimony! If they speak not according to this word, for them there is no daybreak" (Is. 8: 20).

When the Lord Jesus was here on earth as Israel's Messiah, he upbraided the Pharisees and the Sadducees with the charge that although they could tell the signs of the weather, they could not discern "the signs of the times" (Matt. 16: 3). Today the charge against many religious leaders has to be that they do not know the times of the signs—that is, they assume that the present day is just like the period covered by the Gospels and the Acts, and they expect, and claim to have, the same miracles that took place then. The root cause of this error is that they do not cut "in a straight line the word of truth" (2 Tim. 2: 15) and hence fail to realise that the present moment is not one of ***the times of the signs***.

**Distinction and Identification**

In relation to marriage, the Lord Jesus laid down an important principle: "What therefore God has joined together, let not man separate" (Mark 10: 9). By inference and Scriptures such as Gen. 1: 4; Lev. 20: 26 etc. the converse is also true, namely that what God has chosen to separate, men should not try to put together. It is imperative to follow these principles for the right interpretation of the Scriptures. Thus, we must carefully distinguish between:

- the signs and the gifts
- the Jew and the Gentile
- the Kingdom and the Church

and we will see that Scripture identifies:

- the signs with the Jew and the Kingdom
- the gifts with the Christian and the Church

We must note the times when God's testimony is to:

- the Jew alone in the Gospels and the early part of the Acts
- both Jew and Gentile, but with the Jew taking precedence in the latter part of the Acts

Hence if the distinctions and identifications given above are correct, we would expect the signs to be:

- in abundance when the testimony is to the Jew alone
- present, though reduced in number, when the Jew

still has priority in the testimony

• absent, when the testimony is to all men irrespective of race

We must also carefully note the differences between those epistles written:

- during the time of the Acts and
- after the history of the Acts has closed

A major consideration will be the bearing of the truth of the Mystery, the great distinguishing feature of the Church, that completes the Word of God (see Col. 1: 25, 26). This is Jew and Gentile joined together in one body and united to Christ in heaven by the Holy Spirit. Hence while the testimony is:

- to the Jew alone or
- as having first place

the Mystery will remain hidden and form no part of the public testimony. It will not be publicly revealed until the Jew as a nation is set aside in judgment and all distinctions between Jew and Gentile in the Church have gone. Finally, we will see that there were certain gifts that were temporary (some of which were also signs) and that these would be done away "when that which is perfect has come" (1 Cor. 13: 10), whereas other gifts would remain "until we all arrive ... at [the] full–grown man" (Eph. 4: 13).

**The Identification of the Signs with Israel**

It is often forgotten that the Old Testament (OT) is largely the history of one nation—Israel. Only the first 11 chapters of Genesis are used by God to give the history of the world from the creation to the call of Abraham, the rest of the OT (with the exception of Job who was a Gentile) being taken up with Israel. The first two millennia of man's history are dispensed with by God in 11 chapters. Even that brief synopsis is only there in order to bring to light a single nation chosen by God.

Now we are told on the first page of Scripture that the lights in the heavens, apart from dividing between day and night, are "for signs, and for seasons, and for days and years" (Gen. 1: 14), but the only specific sign given by God to all men in those first 11 chapters was the rainbow as "a sign of the covenant between me and the earth" (Gen. 9: 13). God gave that sign to all men as the guarantee that He would never again destroy the earth by a flood. We do not read of any other signs until God called Abraham out with the promise that "I will make of thee a great nation" (Gen. 12: 2). In Genesis, Israel's nationhood was in prospect; in Exodus it became a reality when God delivered Israel from Pharaoh's bondage. It is not without note that of all the signs given throughout the OT, those referred to most often are those given in Egypt at Israel's birth as a nation. ***Hence the signs of Scripture are identified with Israel as a nation and with the Jew as a people***. The Jews could rightly speak of "our signs" (Ps. 74: 9), and Paul could distinguish them from others by saying that "Jews indeed ask for signs, and Greeks seek wisdom" (1 Cor. 1: 22). Throughout the Bible, whether in the OT or the New Testament (NT), not only were the signs for the Jews but ***no man ever gave a sign to that nation who was himself not a Jew***.

# Chapter 2

# The Time of the Signs covered by the Gospels

## Introduction

To say that the OT is the background to the four Gospels seems superfluous and yet many read the Gospels as if there is no link. In particular, Matthew's Gospel is a continuation of the OT. Nonetheless many think that the moment we turn the page from Malachi to Matthew everything changes. There is but ***one*** radical change: Israel's Messiah, the Christ is now here. But why did He come? To set aside the Law? To establish the Church? Faced with this question many a believer would reply with the apostle Paul's words "that Christ Jesus came into the world to save sinners" (1 Tim. 1: 15). This is true but it is not the whole truth for the same Paul also wrote "that Jesus Christ became a minister of [the] circumcision for [the] truth of God, to confirm the promises of the fathers; and that the nations should glorify God for mercy" (Rom. 15: 8, 9). We must not use the former Scripture to weaken or set aside the latter. 1 Tim. 1: 15 is the fulfilment of divine ***purpose***; Rom. 15: 8, 9 is how that purpose was to be effected in the ways of God. ***Primarily***, Christ came to fulfil the OT promises made to Israel and ***then*** to bring in universal blessing. He came firstly to the Jew in answer to the OT Scriptures for it says, "*he* shall save his people from their sins" (Matt. 1: 21) and His people were Israel: "my people the children of Israel" (Ex. 3: 10), not the nations nor the Church that did not yet exist. Again, the Lord said to the woman of Samaria "salvation is of the Jews" (John 4: 22). It was only after He was rejected by Israel and crucified that He became "the Saviour of the world" (v42).

Now if the Lord came initially ***to Israel***, it follows that His testimony was ***for Israel*** as Peter confirms by speaking of the "word which he sent to the sons of Israel" (Acts 10: 36). Indeed, we can go further and say that, initially, Christ came ***exclusively*** to Israel for He himself says "I have not been sent ***save*** to the lost sheep of Israel's house" (Matt.

15: 24—my emphasis). ***Thus, Christ came at first to Israel, to the Jew and to no one else.***

## The Object of the Lord's Coming to Israel

What was the Lord's immediate object in coming to the Jew? We have already had the answer from the Scriptures: He came "to confirm the promises of the fathers" (Rom. 15: 8). Those promises involved the setting up of a universal Kingdom on earth as Paul goes on to say, quoting Is. 11: 10: "There shall be the root of Jesse, and one that arises, to rule over [the] nations" (Rom. 15: 12). This Kingdom was the subject of OT prophecy. It would be universal, embracing all nations (see Ps. 2: 8; 47: 6–8; Dan 7: 14) and Israel would be dominant in it (see Ps. 47: 3; Is. 60: 12). It would be established in power (see Ps. 2: 9) and righteousness (see Ps. 45: 6; Is. 32: 1) and would be a time of universal peace (see Is. 2: 4; Mic. 4: 3). Furthermore, it would be the time when the effects of sin in regard to creation would be undone. We read that the "wolf and the lamb shall feed together, and the lion shall eat straw like the ox; and dust shall be the serpent's meat. They shall not hurt nor destroy in all my holy mountain, saith Jehovah" (Is. 65: 25). The earth would bring forth abundantly and physical defects in man would be eradicated:

> The wilderness and the dry land shall be gladdened; and the desert shall rejoice, and blossom as the rose ... Then the eyes of the blind shall be opened, and the ears of the deaf be unstopped; then shall the lame [man] leap as a hart, and the tongue of the dumb sing: for in the wilderness shall waters break out, and torrents in the desert.
> (Is. 35: 1, 5, 6).

Thus, the effects of sin would be removed. There would be no blind, deaf, lame, or dumb—all disease would be eradicated and even death itself held in check apart from the occasional exception (see Is. 65: 20). Isaiah describes the One who would be King:

> For unto us a child is born, unto us a son is given; and the government shall be upon his shoulder; and his name is called Wonderful, Counsellor, Mighty God,

> Father of Eternity, Prince of Peace. Of the increase of his government and of peace there shall be no end, upon the throne of David and over his kingdom, to establish it, and to uphold it with judgment and with righteousness, from henceforth even for ever.
> (Is. 9: 6, 7).

Again, "And thou, Bethlehem Ephratah, little to be among the thousands of Judah, out of thee shall he come forth unto me [who is] to be Ruler in Israel: whose goings forth are from of old, from the days of eternity" (Micah 5: 2). This Kingdom would have its centre in Israel as the angel said to Mary prior to the Lord's birth:

> ... thou shalt call his name Jesus. *He* shall be great, and shall be called Son of [the] Highest; and [the] Lord God shall give him the throne of David his father; and he shall reign over the house of Jacob for the ages, and of his kingdom there shall not be an end.
> (Luke 1: 31–33).

The question that the magi from the East asked was "Where is the king of the Jews that has been born?" (Matt. 2: 2). When the King's herald, John the Baptist, cried "Repent, for the kingdom of the heavens has drawn nigh" (Matt. 3: 2), there was no astonishment for he had all the characteristics of Elijah who was expected to return before the Messiah came (see Mal. 4: 5). However, the setting up of that Kingdom first required the nation's repentance for their past sins. Accordingly, when the Lord began His testimony, it was in identical words to that of the Baptist: "Repent, for the kingdom of the heavens has drawn nigh" (Matt. 4: 17). ***Thus, Christ came exclusively to Israel as King to establish His Kingdom on earth—provided the nation repented***.

**The Identification of the Messiah**

Now here a very important consideration arises: How would Israel be able to identify the Messiah? 'Ah!' you say, 'That is obvious, they would be able to recognise Him from the description given in the OT'. This is true, but could not an impostor fulfil many of the conditions and characteristics given in the OT? The answer is yes, as Acts 5: 35–37 shows. However, as the Jew throughout his history was given to expect signs (as, for example Is. 7: 10–16), such that, as already noted, Paul could say "Jews indeed ask for signs" (1 Cor. 1: 22), God would give signs that would clinch the identification of the Messiah. How did the Jew know what signs to expect? They would be those that proved that He would establish the Kingdom in power by setting aside all disease and sickness according to Is. 35: 5, 6 and that He had control over death itself. Thus, the prime purpose of the miracles that Christ performed were as signs that pointed Him out to the Jew as the Christ. Their immediate object was not to corroborate His teaching, nor to give relief from suffering (although of course many did that). They were not to show that He was God manifest in flesh (although miracles such as that recorded in Matt. 8: 23–27 did that) and certainly they had nothing to do with the establishment of the Church. ***Their object was to identify and accredit Jesus as the Messiah***. Hence when John the Baptist had doubts as to Jesus being the Christ, the Lord's word was "Go, report to John what ye hear and see. Blind [men] see and lame walk; lepers are cleansed, and deaf hear; and dead are raised" (Matt. 11: 4, 5). Why did the Lord make such a statement? Because He knew that John would be conversant with the prophecy that said, "Then the eyes of the blind shall be opened, and the ears of the deaf be unstopped; then shall the lame [man] leap as a hart, and the tongue of the dumb sing" (Is. 35: 5, 6). Peter's testimony to the Jews in Acts was to "Jesus the Nazaraean, a man borne witness to by God to you by works of power and wonders and signs, which God wrought by him in your midst" (Acts 2: 22).

In relation to our subject, one striking fact regarding John the Baptist is that "John did no sign" (John 10: 41)—in sharp contrast to the Lord about whom the crowd asked, "Will the Christ, when he comes, do more signs than those which this [man] has done?" (John 7: 31). Why was this? So that there was no possibility of identifying John as the Messiah instead of Jesus—a danger that was very real—see John 1: 19–28. ***Thus, the miracles were signs to the Jew that Jesus was the Messiah who would establish the Kingdom in power on earth***. These signs belonged to the Kingdom and had nothing to do with the Church.

### The Gentile Exceptions

If the miracles that the Lord did were signs that He was the Messiah, what about the miracles that He performed for Gentiles? Yes, there are exceptions, and the exceptions, as is often the case, only prove the rule. Take the Canaanitish woman who cried "Have pity on me, Lord, Son of David; my daughter is miserably possessed by a demon" (Matt. 15: 22) using a title, Son of David, that links Christ exclusively to Israel. The response to her plea, expressed in that way, is that "he did not answer her a word" (v23)—which he explains by saying "I have not been sent save to the lost sheep of Israel's house" (v24). Hence, once again, He Himself states that ***His mission was exclusively to Israel***. It was only when this Gentile woman no longer claimed Israel's place, by dropping the title Son of David, and simply owned His authority by saying "Lord, help me" (v25) that she got her request—for He who was Israel's Messiah was also Son of Man and ever cared with the deepest feelings about the awful effects of sin on men. In some contrast to the Canaanitish woman, the Roman centurion who came to plead for his sick servant did not claim Israel's exclusive ground but rightly recognised in the Lord, as in himself, one under authority. Not only was his request granted, but he secured the telling testimony from the Lord that he possessed the very quality that Israel lacked: "Not even in Israel have I found so great faith" (Matt. 8: 10). Consider the Lord in Samaria. When the woman at the well advances Samaria's claim to worship, the Lord states the stark truth "Ye worship ye know not what; we worship what we know, for salvation is of the Jews" (John 4: 22). The phrase "salvation is of the Jews" does not mean that they had priority in salvation but that it was their inherent right (and will be fully realised in the Kingdom)—it belonged to them, not the Gentiles nor the Samaritans. Consequent on His conversation with the woman we are told that the Lord spent two days in Samaria (see John 4: 39–42) but note it well, ***there is no record that He performed any miracles there—for the signs were for the Jews***. Herod the Tetrarch "hoped to see some sign done by him" (Luke 23: 8) but "*he* answered him nothing" (v9). Again, no miracles were performed before Pontius Pilate. Thus, while on occasion Gentiles may have got the benefit of the Lord's miracles, such as those who came out of Syria (see Matt. 4: 24), their object was to identify Him as Messiah to Israel. What about John's Gospel? All the miracles in that Gospel are called signs and we read that "Many other signs therefore also Jesus did before his disciples ... but these are written that ye may believe that Jesus is the Christ, the Son of God" (John 20: 30, 31). Now when ***given***, the signs were ***to the Jew alone***; when "***written***" about, many years later when Israel was set aside in judgment, they were ***to all who read***—the same testimony as to who Jesus is, not just Israel's Messiah, but God's Son.

**Why were the Signs Miracles?**

We must now consider why the signs took the form of miracles of healing, casting out of demons and of raising the dead. The very chapter in the OT that details the signs that the Jew could expect of the Messiah begins with the conditions that will exist when the Kingdom is set up in power:

> The wilderness and the dry land shall be gladdened; and the desert shall rejoice, and blossom as the rose ... They shall see the glory of Jehovah, the excellency of our God ... Be strong, fear not; behold your God: vengeance cometh, the recompense of God! He will come himself, and save you.
> (Is. 35: 1-4).

It goes on to say:

> ***Then*** the eyes of the blind shall be opened, and the ears of the deaf be unstopped; then shall the lame [man] leap as a hart, and the tongue of the dumb sing: for in the wilderness shall waters break out, and torrents in the desert.
> (vs. 5, 6—my emphasis).

The word "Then" clearly places the signs in the Kingdom period and the words "He will come himself, and save you" in v4 refer to Israel and the time of their salvation—their introduction into physical blessing, the proof of the Lord's word that "salvation is of the Jews" (John 4: 22).

The performance of such miracles as signs showed that not only was Jesus the Messiah but the time for the establishment of the Kingdom in power on earth had arrived. In a word, the signs heralded its imminence for the Lord Himself said "if *I* by [the] Spirit of God cast out demons, then indeed the kingdom of God is come upon you" (Matt. 12: 28). Sickness, disease, incapacity, deformity and death were all the outcome of sin. The possession of men by demons was the ultimate proof that men were held in Satan's power. The breaking of that power was the singular proof that God's authority was again being established, namely that the Kingdom of God was being set up in power on earth. ***The signs thus belong to the Kingdom and point to the imminence of its establishment in power on earth***. Again, we read:

> For it is impossible to renew again to repentance those once enlightened, and who have tasted of the heavenly gift, and have been made partakers of [the] Holy Spirit, and have tasted the good word of God, ***and [the] works of power of [the] age to come***. (Heb. 6: 4, 5—my emphasis).

The Hebrew epistle is addressed to Jews and the works of power (miracles) are described as works of power ***of the age to come*** (the Kingdom) showing that without question the setting for the miracles is the Kingdom. Yet another Scripture that ties up the thought of salvation, the signs and the Kingdom is in the same epistle where we read of the "great salvation, which, having had its commencement in being spoken [of] by the Lord ..." (Heb. 2: 3). What was this great salvation? Most would limit it to the salvation of the soul, but this is not true for when the salvation of the soul is in view in Hebrews, it is stated as such by the writer (see Heb. 10: 39). Earlier we read "For he has not subjected to angels the habitable world which is to come, ***of which we speak***" (Heb. 2: 5—my emphasis).[1] The subject that the writer is speaking of is the world to come, the millennium, the Kingdom. Hence the "great salvation" is the full and final thought of salvation realised when Christ sets up the Kingdom here in power and men are finally and fully delivered from the power of Satan—when the great source of evil will be bound "a thousand years ... that he should not any more deceive the nations until the thousand years were completed" (Rev. 20: 2, 3). It is the moment when "Christ ... shall appear to those that look for him the second time without sin for salvation" (Heb. 9: 28) and they shall live and reign "with the Christ a thousand years" (Rev. 20: 4).

---

[1] While this clause is often taken to mean that the world to come is the topic of Christian conversation (or should be), it is really the general theme and background to the apostle's teaching (see Heb. 1: 8, 13 where v13 is a quotation from Ps. 110—a psalm that clearly speaks of the reign of Christ in His Kingdom in the world to come).

**The Continuance of the Signs**

While the Lord's rejection by the Jews is viewed by John in his Gospel as almost immediate, Matthew in particular (as written primarily with the Jew in mind) traces out that rejection in its detail. The signs did not cease when the clouds of rejection first began to gather, but continued right up to the point when the Lord was apprehended in Gethsemane. In Matt. 13 (see also Mark 4) when His rejection was clear, He began to veil His ministry in parables and detailed the form that the Kingdom would take throughout the period of His rejection and absence. In verses 13-15 He quotes the prophecy that pronounced judgment on the Jewish nation:

> And he said, Go; and thou shalt say unto this people, Hearing ye shall hear and shall not understand, and seeing ye shall see and shall not perceive. Make the heart of this people fat, and make their ears heavy, and blind their eyes; lest they see with their eyes, and hear with their ears, and understand with their heart, and be converted, and healed. (Is. 6: 9, 10).

This Scripture, which would soon be fulfilled, is quoted again at the end of the Lord's ministry (see John 12: 40) where we read "though he had done so many signs before them, they believed not on him, that the word of the prophet Esaias which he said might be fulfilled" (vs. 37, 38). It is quoted for the final time by Paul in Rome to the leaders of the dispersion in Acts 28: 26, 27. However, in spite of all this we find in Matt. 21: 1–11 the Lord still riding into Jerusalem, thereby formally presenting Himself as the Christ in fulfilment of Zech. 9: 9. The result was His crucifixion. ***Thus, the miracles did not immediately cease when the Lord was rejected but in grace continued until He was crucified***.

**Summary**

I have sought to establish the following points from the Scriptures:

- Christ came initially to the Jew and to no one else
- He came to establish the Kingdom on earth as prophesied in the OT

- The purpose of the signs was to identify Jesus as the Messiah to the Jews
- The signs were miracles to show that He had the power to set up the Kingdom
- The signs showed that the setting up of the Kingdom in power on earth was imminent
- Even after the Lord was rejected by Israel, the signs continued until He was crucified

# Chapter 3

# The Continuation of the Signs during the Lord's Absence

## Introduction

The Jews had crucified their Messiah. Would God immediately set the nation aside in judgment? No, for the Lord had prayed "Father, forgive them, for they know not what they do" (Luke 23: 34). God's testimony would ultimately go out universally "to all the creation" (Mark 16: 15) and "to all the nations" (Luke 24: 47) but only in the specific order of "Jerusalem, and in all Judaea and Samaria, and to the end of the earth" (Acts 1: 8) and "beginning at Jerusalem" (Luke 24: 47). Thus, in wondrous grace the testimony would be to the Jew first and in the very city where the Lord was crucified. As the testimony was to continue to the Jew, and as signs are for the Jews, we would expect the signs to continue. However, as seen in our next Scripture, the situation for the Jew was critical and extremely grave.

## The Bearing of Hebrews 2 on Signs

Although the exact date of Hebrews is uncertain (as are the exact dates of all the NT books), it was certainly written before Jerusalem fell to Titus in AD 70 (for Heb. 13: 14 assumes that the city is still standing) and most probably within the period of the Acts. Those written to were Jews and the writer asks the solemn question:

> ... how shall *we* escape if we have been negligent of so great salvation, which, having had its commencement in being spoken [of] by the Lord, has been confirmed to us by those who have heard; God bearing, besides, witness with [them] to [it], both by signs and wonders, and various acts of power, and distributions of [the] Holy Spirit, according to his will?

> For he has not subjected to angels the habitable world which is to come, of which we speak. (Heb. 2: 3–5).

We have already seen that the comparison of v3 with v5 shows us that this great salvation was not limited to the soul but involved the setting up of the Kingdom in power in the world to come. Let us now look further at these words. This great salvation "had its commencement in being spoken [of] by the Lord" (as in Acts 1: 3) and so if it ***began*** with Him, it must have been ***continued*** by others confirming what the Lord had said. Who were they? Did they include Paul? No, for he always contrasts himself with the twelve, for example, saying that the Lord "appeared for many days to those who had come up with him from Galilee to Jerusalem, who are now his witnesses to the people. And *we* declare unto you ..." (Acts 13: 31, 32). They were "those who have heard" (Heb. 2: 3), that is the twelve apostles and possibly others who had been with the Lord throughout His ministry—they were certainly not any persons alive today. To whom did they confirm this great salvation? To Gentiles? To the Church? No! But "to us" (v3), that is, to those written to in the book of Hebrews—Jews. They were not alone in their testimony for God bore witness with them to it. How? "both by signs and wonders, and various acts of power, and distributions of [the] Holy Spirit, according to his will" (v4). These verses give us the reason for the continuance of the signs: to bear witness to those who confirmed the Lord's testimony. Thus, if the signs in the Gospels were to identify Jesus as the Christ and to show that the establishment of the Kingdom in power was imminent (if Israel had repented), then the continuance of the same signs (with the addition of tongues) was God's witness to the apostles' confirmation of the Lord's testimony on the selfsame theme. Hence no one can confirm the Lord's ministry today. Why? ***Because there is no one today who has heard Him***! To claim, as some may, that they have seen and heard the Lord in visions and dreams will not do. Paul could rightly claim that the Lord "appeared to *me* also" (1 Cor. 15: 8) but he could not, and did not, claim to have heard the Lord on earth. Those who have heard Him have gone and the signs have gone with them.

Again, as the signs were God's witness to the continuation of the testimony of the great salvation which embraces the Kingdom of God in power, ***then if the establishment of the Kingdom in power is***

***delayed indefinitely and that testimony ceases, then God's witness of signs will also cease***.

## The Signs of Mark 16

While Heb. 2: 3–5 is an historical synopsis of the continuation of the signs during the Lord's absence, Mark 16: 15–20 is a prophetic synopsis for the same period given by the Lord Himself. This is a key Scripture for those who claim that tongues, healings and the like continue today for they quote:

> And these signs shall follow those that have believed: in my name they shall cast out demons; they shall speak with new tongues; they shall take up serpents; and if they should drink any deadly thing it shall not injure them; they shall lay hands upon the infirm, and they shall be well.
> (Mark 16: 17, 18).

Certainly, the Lord does say in v17 "these signs shall follow those that have believed". However, this verse does not say that these signs shall follow those that ***shall believe***, nor that these signs shall follow those that ***believe*** but these signs shall follow those that ***have believed***. The tense of the verb "believed" is not the future, nor the present but the past.[2] It does not refer to those who would believe at that time, or in the future, ***but is limited to those who had already believed when the Lord spoke*** and thus has no reference to any future believers. Hence the Pentecostal/ Charismatic claim to sign–gifts is not warranted from these verses. Continuing on, v19 says "The Lord therefore, after he had spoken to them ..." and clearly in the context of the chapter, these can only be the eleven. Hence when it says in the following verse "they, going forth, preached everywhere, the Lord working with [them], and confirming the word by the signs following upon [it]" (v20), ***it must be***

[2] The grammar of the Greek is enlightening here. The clause "that have believed" is an aorist participle (*pisteusasi*). Now normally where the aorist is used (as in v16 for "believed") it indicates just the fact apart from time, but when it depends on a main verb, such as "shall follow" in v17, we are told by scholars that it refers to an action ***that has already taken place***. Thus, in the words of one Greek authority "*pisteusasi* is in the aor. tense indicating those who at some time in the past had believed" (see Zodhiates, S. *The Complete Word Study Dictionary New Testament*, AMG Publishers 1992, p376).

***the eleven who fulfilled the Lord's prophecy*** that "these signs shall follow those that have believed" (v17). This is entirely in keeping with the verses in Hebrews namely, that the testimony "has been confirmed to us ***by those who have heard***" (Heb. 2: 3, 4—my emphasis). Furthermore, the word translated "confirming" in Mark 16: 20 is the same Greek word used in Heb. 2: 3, adding further weight to the point that those who performed the signs recorded in the Acts were largely the apostles and not believers in general. I say this because when we come to the history of the fulfilment of Mark 16: 17 given in Acts, we have this very significant fact: nowhere is the performance of miracles and signs in the publication of the testimony associated with believers in general ***as such. It is always identified with the apostles***. I will enlarge on this point later. Hence these signs were not to confirm the faith of those that believed, either to themselves or to others, but to confirm the testimony of the twelve. ***Thus, I repeat, the continuance of signs to the present day cannot be claimed from these verses in Mark 16***.

Now the detail of this Scripture will help us further. We read:

> And these signs shall follow those that have believed: in my name they shall cast out demons; they shall speak with new tongues; they shall take up serpents; and if they should drink any deadly thing it shall not injure them; they shall lay hands upon the infirm, and they shall be well.
> (Mark 16: 17, 18).

There are five signs listed here. Four of them were exercised by the Lord's disciples, either the twelve or the seventy, in the Gospels. They cast out demons (see, for example, Luke 10: 17), they healed the sick (see, for example, Matt. 10: 8) and the statement "and nothing shall in anywise injure you" (Luke 10: 19) would embrace the words "they shall take up serpents; and if they should drink any deadly thing it shall not injure them" (Mark 16: 18). Thus, the signs listed in Mark 16 were all experienced by the disciples with one important exception and that exception is the speaking with new tongues. Why were all the other signs exercised in the Gospels but not the sign of tongues? Surely this fact alone indicates that tongues is a distinctive sign, having a peculiar character? Hence before we go any further, we must look at the Scriptures that speak of tongues.

**Summary**

I have sought to establish the following points from the Scriptures:

- The testimony begun by the Lord in the Gospels was continued by the apostles
- This testimony was to the identification of Jesus as the Christ and the promise of the Kingdom if the Jews repented
- The signs exercised in the Gospels would continue with the addition of the new sign of tongues
- These signs were to be performed by those who had heard the Lord on earth
- These signs would be the divine confirmation of the testimony of the apostles
- Mark 16 provides no Biblical warrant for the continuance of signs today

# Chapter 4

# The Time for the Peculiar Sign of Tongues

## Introduction

If there is one sign that is claimed more frequently than any other today, it is tongues. Such dominance makes it unique. However, more importantly, it is also unique in the Scriptures. For it is the one sign that is absent in the Gospels but present in Acts. This striking fact must not be ignored. Indeed, it is the key to understanding the objective of tongues. Being a sign, like the other miracles, it is primarily for the Jew, but unlike the other signs, being absent from the Gospels it does not point to Jesus as the Christ. ***Hence tongues must have a peculiar and distinct significance***.

Like healing and prophecy, the sign of tongues was also a gift (see 1 Cor. 12: 8–10) and a cursory read of 1 Cor. 12–14 shows that the exercise of tongues was made much of in the Corinthian assembly. However, while Paul does not prohibit its exercise, ***he does ban its public use in the assembly unless there is one present who can interpret*** (see 1 Cor. 14: 26–28). Without interpretation, the exercise of the gift of tongues was valueless in the assembly as it provided no edification to those who heard but did not understand (see 1 Cor. 14: 6–17). The Corinthians' use of tongues showed that they were immature. Their attitude was childish and so Paul exhorts them not to be children in their thinking but full–grown men (note the identification of children with tongues—a fact I shall take up later). This brings to the Apostle's mind an incident from the OT which he quotes, using it as the basis for his conclusion: "So that tongues are for a sign, not to those who believe, but to unbelievers" (v22). While in the setting of the assembly, tongues were a gift, we are told authoritatively here that their ***actual purpose was as a sign***. But a sign to whom and of what? A sign "not to those who believe, but to unbelievers" (v22). Thus, tongues have no ***significance*** to Christians, for they are believers. The significance of tongues is to unbelievers.

But who are the unbelievers? Paul's conclusion as to tongues in v22 comes from his quotation of Is. 28: 11, 12 in the previous verse where he says "By people of other tongues, and by strange lips, will I speak to ***this people***; and neither thus will they hear me, saith the Lord." (1 Cor. 14: 21—my emphasis).[3] Now Isaiah 28 has nothing whatsoever to do with Gentiles, but everything to do with the unbelieving nation of Israel. The words "this people" in Isaiah 28: 11 refer to them. Hence like the other signs, tongues are for the Jew. This is further strengthened as it is in this very epistle that Paul says, "Since Jews indeed ask for signs" (1 Cor. 1: 22). What then is the significance of this sign and Paul's quotation of Is. 28 in the previous verse? To understand that we must go back to the OT, to the prophetic warnings that God gave to Israel.

**The Significance of Tongues**

Centuries before the Lord Jesus came, Moses had warned Israel that if they failed to keep Jehovah's commandments then "Jehovah will bring a nation against thee from afar, from the end of the earth, like as the eagle flieth, a nation ***whose tongue thou understandest not***" (Deut. 28: 49—my emphasis). This warning was repeated by Isaiah (see Is. 28) largely for the ten tribes of the northern kingdom (although not excluding Judah) in view of the approach of the Assyrian hordes to the city of Samaria in Ephraim. It was repeated again by Jeremiah for the two tribes under Judah at a later date in view of the approach of the Babylonians to the walls of Jerusalem: "Behold, I bring a nation upon you from afar, house of Israel, saith Jehovah: it is a mighty nation, it is an ancient nation, ***a nation whose language thou knowest not, neither understandest thou what they say***" (Jer. 5: 15—my emphasis. Indeed, read the whole chapter). In each case the significance is identical: when they heard the sound of tongues that they did not understand, languages foreign to their ears, they would know that God's judgment was imminent. In each case they lost their national

---

[3] While "those who believe" were both Jews and Gentiles, "unbelievers" were Jews. I do not mean, of course, that there were no Gentile unbelievers but that the Jews were in the vanguard of unbelief and ***thus represented that unbelief***. Opposition to the testimony in the Acts was from them. Of some 35 examples of opposition recorded in Acts, five may be attributed to the Gentiles, the rest to the Jews. In Acts 13: 45 we read "But the Jews ... contradicted the things said by Paul" and this sort of statement, in contrast to Gentile interest in God's Word, occurs again and again in Acts (see Acts 13: 50; 14: 2, 4; 14: 19; 17: 5, 13; 28: 19).

identity. The ten tribes were taken captive to Assyria and the two tribes were later carried away to Babylon. Thus, the significance of tongues in the NT was God's impending judgment on the unbelieving nation by Gentiles following the crucifixion of their Messiah, as prophesied in detail by the Lord in Luke 21: 5, 6, 20, 24. This was fulfilled to the letter when Titus sacked Jerusalem in AD 70, after which Israel ceased to exist as a nation for centuries. In Isaiah's day, they would not listen to the simple words of the prophet:

> Whom shall he teach knowledge? and whom shall he make to understand the report? Them that are weaned from the milk, withdrawn from the breasts? For [it is] precept upon precept, precept upon precept; line upon line, line upon line; here a little, there a little .... For with stammering lips and a strange tongue will he speak to this people.
> (Is. 28: 9–11).

The Corinthians in Paul's day were just as foolish: "Brethren, be not children in [your] minds, but in malice be babes; but in [your] minds be [grown [men]" (1 Cor. 14: 20). This national stubbornness of Israel—expressed in Paul's quotation "By people of other tongues, and by strange lips, will I speak to this people; and ***neither thus will they hear me, saith the Lord***. So that tongues are for a sign, not to those who believe, but to unbelievers" (vs. 21, 22—my emphasis)—is spoken of elsewhere. For example, "God has given to them a spirit of slumber, eyes not to see, and ears not to hear, unto this day" (Rom. 11: 8).

In parallel with Israel's judgmental setting aside is the introduction of the Gentiles to the blessings promised to Abraham (see Gen 12: 3) as Paul argues out in Romans 10 and 11 (see particularly Rom. 11: 11–21).[4] Indeed, in his argument there Paul actually quotes Is 28: 16 (from the Septuagint) "For the scripture says, No one believing on him shall be ashamed" (Rom. 10: 11) which he uses to introduce the words "For there is no difference of Jew and Greek; for the same Lord of all [is] rich towards all that call upon him. For every one whosoever, who shall call on the name of the Lord, shall be saved" (Rom. 10: 12, 13).

---

[4] Incidentally, Romans 10 and 11 have nothing to do with the Church as such but present–day Israel in contradistinction to the Gentiles.

Thus the sign of tongues was God's final warning to the Jew after the crucifixion of the Messiah of impending national judgment[5] and of blessing to the nations. Hence the sign of tongues is absent from the Gospels and was only to be exercised when the twelve went forth after the Lord had ascended. We will now examine the three definite occasions in Acts where tongues were used to see if they bear this out.

**Tongues in Acts 2**

Tongues was the very first sign given in Acts and was commensurate with the descent of the Holy Spirit. We read that:

> And there appeared to them parted tongues, as of fire, and it sat upon each one of them. And they were all filled with [the] Holy Spirit, and began to speak with other tongues as the Spirit gave to them to speak forth.
> (Acts 2: 3, 4)

It was the rumour of this marvel spreading that drew the multitude, "Jews, pious men, from every nation of those under heaven" (v5). These were all Jews that were gathered to the Feast of Pentecost (interestingly, we are told by scholars that of all the feasts, the Feast of Pentecost drew more of the Jewish dispersion to Jerusalem that any other). Now the words "are not all these who are speaking Galilaeans? and how do *we* hear [them] each in our own dialect in which we have been born ... we hear them speaking in our own tongues the great things of God" (vs. 7-11) clearly prove that these tongues were real, ethnic, grammatical languages. It was impossible for them to have been the ecstatic ungrammatical utterances practised today among many in the Pentecostal/Charismatic movement.[6] The report of this sign of tongues and the details of Peter's subsequent preaching would go to the four corners of the earth when these Jews returned home from the feast.

Now Peter in his preaching invokes the prophet Joel as the basis for

---

[5] It is a well–known fact that the first mention of anything in the Bible often indicates its meaning throughout. The first mention of language is in Gen. 11: 1–9 on the occasion of the building of the tower of Babel. "Jehovah there confounded the language of the whole earth" (v9) in ***divine judgment*** for what they did.

[6] See Appendix 1.

what was taking place where the prophet speaks of the day of the Lord—which is always the time of judgment (see Is. 2: 12; 13: 6, 9; 34: 8 etc.). Nonetheless Peter terminates his quotation from Joel with the words "And it shall be that whosoever shall call upon the name of [the] Lord shall be saved" (Acts 2: 21). While Peter addresses this verse to Jews alone, it is ***the very same verse*** that Paul also uses in Rom. 10: 13 to argue the truth of his previous verse "For there is no difference of Jew and Greek; for the same Lord of all [is] rich towards all that call upon him. For every one whosoever, who shall call on the name of the Lord, shall be saved" (vs. 12, 13). Hence blessing was to go out to both Jew and Gentile on the same basis, the only difference being that it would go out to the Jew first. So, the exercise of the sign of tongues on the day of Pentecost was used to warn the Jews of their impending judgment on the one hand, and of blessing to all who would call on the name of the Lord on the other. The Jews had crucified their Messiah as Peter testifies (see Acts 2: 34–36) - what could they now do? Peter's reply is:

> ... Repent, and be baptised, each one of you, in the name of Jesus Christ, for remission of sins, and ye will receive the gift of the Holy Spirit. For to you is the promise and to your children, and to all who [are] afar off, as many as [the] Lord our God may call.
> (Acts 2: 38, 39).

**Tongues in Acts 10**

The second occasion[7] of tongues in Acts is in chapter 10 when Peter and six Jews went to Cornelius, a Gentile. We read:

> While Peter was yet speaking these words the Holy Spirit fell upon all those who were hearing the word. And the faithful of the circumcision were astonished,

---

[7] Some claim that tongues were exercised when the Samaritans were converted. This is argued from the fact that it says that "Simon, ***having seen*** that by the laying on of the hands of the apostles the [Holy] Spirit was given" (Acts 8: 18—my emphasis). The assumption being that there must have been some visible evidence to Simon of the gift of the Holy Spirit and that this evidence was the Samaritans speaking in tongues. Even if the Samaritans did speak in tongues, it would not militate against the arguments put forward above, but as the Scriptures do not say so, the matter need not be considered.

> as many as came with Peter, that upon the nations also the gift of the Holy Spirit was poured out: for they heard them speaking with tongues and magnifying God.
> (Acts. 10: 44–46).

Clearly, these verses show that tongues were the evidence, not to Cornelius and his household, but to Peter and the Jews that the Gentiles had received the Holy Spirit just as the Jews had done at Pentecost. Hence later, when Peter went up to Jerusalem, "they of the circumcision contended with him, saying, Thou wentest in to men uncircumcised and hast eaten with them" (Acts 11: 2, 3) and Peter responds to this challenge by detailing what had happened saying:

> And as I began to speak, the Holy Spirit fell upon them even as upon us also at the beginning. And I remembered the word of the Lord, how he said, John baptised with water, but *ye* shall be baptised with [the] Holy Spirit. If then God has given them the same gift as also to us when we had believed on the Lord Jesus Christ, who indeed was *I* to be able to forbid God?
> (Acts. 11: 15–17).

Thus, speaking with tongues was the proof to the Jew that God had given the Gentiles the gift of the Holy Spirit. The conclusion of the believing Jews was that then indeed "God has to the nations also granted repentance to life" (v18). ***If the Gentiles were brought into blessing on the same ground as the Jew, it could only mean that Israel's unique national place of blessing was about to be set aside.***

**Tongues in Acts 19**

The final occurrence of tongues in Acts is in chapter 19 where we read of disciples who, in some way, came to the attention of Paul. Whether they had actually been baptised by John the Baptist in Judaea and had later moved to Ephesus or had become disciples of John as a result of the testimony of Apollos and had subsequently been baptised in Ephesus, does not matter. The latter is more probable as this incident immediately follows our introduction to Apollos in Acts 18. What is certain is that Ephesus had two groups of Jews: those who had accepted John's testimony and those who had either rejected it or were indifferent to it.

Now John's testimony was "[the] baptism of repentance for remission of sins" (Mark 1: 4). Not only did he preach the coming Kingdom but warned of "the coming wrath" (Matt. 3: 7) and of the setting aside of Israel with the words: "And do not think to say within yourselves, We have Abraham for [our] father; for I say unto you, that God ***is able of these stones to raise up children to Abraham*** " (v9—my emphasis). He testified to the Jews of the Christ that "*he* shall baptise you with [the] Holy Spirit and fire" (v11). Now these 12 or so disciples did not receive the Holy Spirit until Paul had laid his hands upon them. There is a parallel here to the reception of the Holy Spirit by the Samaritans in Acts 8, but for a different reason. If the Holy Spirit had come upon these disciples at Ephesus without the laying on of Paul's hands, then they would have been seen to have been no different to those Jews at Ephesus who had not accepted John's testimony. In identifying himself with them by laying his hands upon them, Paul was certifying the truth of John's testimony to the rest of the Jews. The Holy Spirit thus sealed Paul's identification by coming upon them through the medium of Paul's hands. Hence the subsequent speaking with tongues and prophesying showed to the rest of the Jewish community that the Baptist's warning of coming judgment upon their nation was true. The statement "And entering into the synagogue" (Acts 19: 8) clearly shows that this incident took place in the near vicinity of the synagogue when a meeting was about to take place[8] and thus in the presence of unbelieving Jews. Finally, Paul's subsequent testimony to the rest of the Jews in that place was "concerning the kingdom of God" (v8) which, as we shall see later, is the testimony throughout Acts.

Thus in all three incidents involving tongues in Acts, we have Jews present and the universal testimony of this sign is a warning to them that unless there was national repentance then they would lose their distinctive place and that blessing would go out to the Gentiles instead.

---

[8] The words are not 'And going to the synagogue' which would imply that the synagogue was some distance away but "And entering into the synagogue" (Acts 19: 8). This shows that they were about to enter before this incident took place and that they would only do so if other Jews were there.

## Summary

I have sought to establish the following points from the Scriptures:

- The sign of tongues was only given by the Lord Jesus after His crucifixion and resurrection
- Hence it must have a peculiar significance
- Like the other signs, the sign of tongues was for the Jews
- Paul's quotation from the OT in 1 Cor. 14 shows that tongues were given as a final warning to the Jews that if they still continued to reject their Messiah, the nation would be set aside in judgment
- Again, the references in the OT and the first example of the exercise of the sign in Acts 2, show that tongues were real ethnic languages
- The use of the sign in Acts 10 and 19 also shows that tongues heralded the national judgment on the Jew and the advent of the testimony to the Gentiles

# Chapter 5

# The Time that the Testimony was Restricted to Jerusalem (Acts 1–7)

## Introduction

Having dealt with the important sign of tongues in detail, we are now in a position to look at the history of signs as presented in the book of Acts. So far as our subject is concerned, we may divide the book into two: the time that the testimony is restricted to Jerusalem and the time that the testimony goes beyond that city. The first seven chapters of Acts detail the history of the testimony in Jerusalem. That testimony is exclusively to the Jews. It is to Jesus as the Messiah, the Christ, in relation to the Kingdom. Hence, we will find that the apostles' testimony is confirmed by an abundance of signs from God. While the Church is formed in Acts 2, it is nonetheless entirely Jewish—there is not a single Gentile in it. Thus, there is no hint as to the truth of the Mystery. Luke in his opening words makes it crystal clear (see Acts 1: 1, 2) that this history is a continuation of the history that he had previously given in his Gospel. Hence the prime testimony throughout Acts is to the Kingdom.

## The Continuance of the Testimony of the Gospels

In the opening verses of Acts, we find the risen Lord speaking to the eleven during the forty days that He was on earth, not about the Church, but about the Kingdom of God (see Acts 1: 3). The disciples thus ask, "is it at this time that thou restorest the kingdom to Israel?" (v6). Clearly, this is not the Kingdom in its spiritual aspect as "righteousness, and peace, and joy in [the] Holy Spirit" (Rom. 14: 17) but the Kingdom as presented in the OT. Note that there is no doubt in their minds as to its future restoration—the only uncertainty with them is as to when. Israel was not yet set aside for, as already said, the

Lord had prayed on the cross "Father, forgive them, for they know not what they do" (Luke 23: 34). Thus, the testimony is still to be to the Jew and that testimony is of the Kingdom. Accordingly, once the Lord had ascended, we read:

> It is necessary therefore, that of the men who have assembled with us all [the] time in which the Lord Jesus came in and went out among us, beginning from the baptism of John until the day in which he was taken up from us, one of these should be a witness with us of his resurrection.
> (Acts 1: 21, 22).

Peter bases the necessary replacement of Judas on Ps. 109: 8. Why was it necessary? The disciples were obliged to do this because they knew that when the Kingdom is established on earth, twelve thrones are to be occupied by twelve apostles judging in Israel as the Lord had clearly told them, saying "*ye* also shall sit on twelve thrones, judging the twelve tribes of Israel" (Matt. 19: 28). Again, in the Jerusalem yet to come, there will be twelve foundations, "and on them twelve names of the twelve apostles of the Lamb" (Rev. 21: 14). Hence a twelfth apostle must be chosen to take the place of Judas. His replacement had nothing whatsoever to do with the Church ***but had everything to do with the imminence of the Kingdom***. Accordingly, the ***Jewish*** practice of casting lots was employed for this election.

On the day of Pentecost in Acts 2 the very first sign recorded is that of tongues and it was a sign to all the Jews gathered at Jerusalem for the feast. It attracted them to the disciples and was a sign of warning of the coming judgment on the nation if they continued to reject God's testimony to Jesus as the Christ. Now if you compare Acts 1: 15 and Acts 2: 1 with Acts 2: 14 you will see that while all those who had gathered spoke with tongues, ***it was just the eleven who stood up with Peter to testify*** when he delivered his address in the local language. He substantiates what had taken place from Joel 2: 28 and reminded them of "Jesus the Nazaraean, a man borne witness to by God to you by works of power and wonders and signs, which God wrought by him in your midst, as yourselves know" (Acts 2: 22), and declared that "God has made him, this Jesus whom *ye* have crucified, both Lord and Christ" (v36). ***Hence, we have the testimony continuing exclusively to the Jews, identifying Jesus as the Christ, confirmed now***

***by the sign of tongues warning of coming judgment if they continue to reject Him***. Notice too that those who accept Peter's word must make exactly the same response as that demanded by John the Baptist in his announcement of the imminence of the Kingdom—repentance and baptism. Three thousand responded positively, were added to the Church[9] and were thus "saved from this ***perverse generation***" (v40—my emphasis). Note the words carefully. They did not separate from the nation and give up their Jewish identity—for Israel was not as yet set aside as a nation in judgment—but they did separate from those in the nation who continued to reject Jesus as the Messiah. They were in the Church and indwelt of the Holy Spirit, but the truth of the Mystery was still hidden for Scripture does not, as yet, speak of a single Gentile believer. At this time, we read "And fear was upon every soul, and many wonders and signs took place through the apostles' means" (v43). These signs were limited to the apostles, to the twelve—again showing the true meaning of Mark 16: 17. Note too that it speaks of many wonders and signs. ***Once Jerusalem, the kernel of Judaism, has refused this testimony, such a multiplicity of signs will never again be repeated***.

In chapter three we have the second sign, the miracle of the healing of the impotent man. Not only do the rulers class this as a sign (see Acts 4: 16) but the inspired writer speaks of it in exactly the same way saying that "the man on whom this sign of healing had taken place was above forty years old" (v22). The significance is that the One in whose name this man was ***physically*** healed was the One who was waiting to heal His people ***spiritually*** likewise—if they repented. Peter, addressing the rulers of the nation, puts their sin down as a sin of ignorance so that the Lord's prayer on the cross for forgiveness could take place and then goes on to say:

> Repent therefore and be converted, for the blotting out of your sins, so that times of refreshing may come from [the] presence of the Lord, and he may send Jesus Christ, who was foreordained for you, whom heaven indeed must receive till [the] times of [the]

---

[9] The word for Church or Assembly in Greek is *ekklesia* which simply means those called out and, ***in itself***, it has no ecclesiastical meaning.

> restoring of all things, of which God has spoken by the mouth of his holy prophets since time began.
> (Acts 3: 19–21).

***Hence the Lord would return and establish the Kingdom if the nation repented***. Peter and John are then apprehended, providing Peter with the opportunity of addressing the rulers of the nation using the sign of the healing of the lame man to underline his testimony to the resurrection of Jesus as Israel's Saviour. All to no avail. Subsequent to their release, the prayer to the Lord to stretch "out thy hand to heal, and that signs and wonders take place through the name of thy holy servant Jesus" (Acts 4: 30) brought the result that "the place in which they were assembled shook, and they were all filled with the Holy Spirit, and spoke the word of God with boldness" (v31). While the preaching appears to have been the privilege of all, the performance of the signs is ***limited to the apostles*** for we read "and with great power did the apostles give witness of the resurrection of the Lord Jesus, and great grace was upon them all" (v33) and "by the hands of the apostles were many signs and wonders done among the people" (Acts 5: 12). I must ask you again to note the language carefully: "many signs and wonders". ***Once the testimony leaves Jerusalem, words like these expressing the abundance of signs will never be recorded again in Scripture***. Peter's second appearance before the rulers does not change their attitude and the testimony continues in the city of "the glad tidings that Jesus [was] the Christ" (v42).

## God's Final Testimony to Jerusalem

God's final testimony to Jerusalem is by a unique vessel—Stephen. He was not one of the twelve and he was not an apostle. He was not even an indigenous Jew but a Hellenist—a Greek Jew (this is shown by the fact that the murmuring in Acts 6: 1 was of the Hellenists against the Hebrew Jews and not the other way round.) He was one of the seven chosen by the disciples to serve tables so that the twelve apostles could concentrate on "prayer and the ministry of the word" (v4). Yet we have no record given by the Holy Spirit of this table service by any of the seven. What the Spirit of God ***does*** record is the spiritual service of Stephen in Jerusalem and of Philip in Samaria (see Acts 8: 4–40)—for while the former gave the final testimony to Jerusalem before it went to the Gentiles, Philip gave the initial testimony to Samaria. The choice of the seven is confirmed, after prayer, by the laying on of the hands of the apostles. Why was this? This was an OT practice and always indicates identification and sometimes the bestowal of authority and the donation of something. Hence by the laying on of the hands of Moses, Joshua was identified with Moses, filled with the spirit of wisdom and given the authority of Judaism's apostle (see Heb. 3: 1, 2): "And Joshua the son of Nun was filled with the spirit of wisdom, for Moses had laid his hands upon him; and the children of Israel hearkened unto him, and did as Jehovah had commanded Moses" (Deut. 34: 9). Similarly in the NT we read that Timothy was reminded by the apostle Paul to "rekindle the gift of God which is in thee by the putting on of my hands" (2 Tim. 1: 6). Stephen, Philip and the rest of the seven[10] were thus identified with the apostles and apostolic authority was conferred upon them by the laying on of hands. Thus it is no surprise to find Stephen now, and Philip later, performing signs which, as far as the record of Scripture goes, were the exclusive domain of the apostles: "Stephen, full of grace and power, wrought wonders and great signs among the people" (Acts 6: 8).

My reader may like to note that, as far as the record in Acts is concerned, ***every miracle performed in Jerusalem is described by the Holy Spirit as a sign and Jerusalem's last signs were given by Stephen***. This remarkable man is used to give the final cutting testimony to the rulers in Jerusalem. His last words of testimony "Lo, I behold the heavens opened, and the Son of man[11] standing at the right hand of God" (Acts 7: 56) show that the Lord in standing was ready to return to His people, but the designation of Son of Man and the fact that the testimony was given by a Hellenist, also show that the blessing

---

[10] Note that these men when they are mentioned later in Acts 21: 8 are not referred to as "ministers" (or "deacons" as in the AV), even though they were chosen to serve tables as such, but as "the seven" indicating that they were viewed as a distinct and peculiar body, well known as such. A parallel may be drawn with these seven and the seventy of Luke 10: 1–24. When the work was too great for the twelve, a further seventy were appointed by the Lord and sent out by Him with similar instructions to those given to the twelve. The seventy performed similar miracles to the twelve but they are never called apostles. While their appointment and service clearly linked them with the twelve, they are never accorded the distinctive place of the twelve. Thus, likewise, while the seven are never called apostles, they are identified with the apostles by the laying on of hands and accordingly performed the signs of the apostles.

[11] As Son of David, the Lord stands in relation to Israel as their Messiah (see Matt. 1: 1; 12: 23; 22: 42); as Son of Man, He stands in relation to all men as Man. The expression Son of Man first appears in Ps. 8: 4. The setting of Ps. 8 and its quotation in Heb. 2: 6–8 shows that it is the Lord's title in connection with His universal dominion over the earth.

subsequently is not going to be limited to Jerusalem and Israel. The nation's response is to murder him as they murdered his Master. However, in the amazing ways of God, the one that assisted in that murder is to be apprehended, converted, and become the prime vessel to take God's testimony beyond the bounds of Israel.

**Summary**

I have sought to establish the following points from the Scriptures:

- As in the Gospels, the testimony in Jerusalem was to the Jew and no one else
- The signs were to confirm the word of the apostles, giving the same testimony as in the Gospels, that Jesus was the Christ
- This period of the Acts saw the apostles perform a multitude of signs for the Jews, just as the Lord and the apostles did in the period of the Gospels
- The Lord was ready to return and establish the Kingdom in power if the nation would repent
- The exercise of the sign of tongues was the warning of coming judgment on the nation and of blessing going out to the Gentiles
- Stephen, Philip and the rest of the "seven" (Acts 6: 3) were identified with the apostles by the laying on of hands
- God's final testimony in Jerusalem to the Jews was to the Son of Man by Stephen, a Hellenist, showing that the testimony was about to go to the Gentiles

# Chapter 6

# The Time that the Testimony went beyond Jerusalem (Acts 8–28)

## Introduction

It has often been said that the book of Acts is a transitional book, being the bridge between the Gospels and the epistles. This is particularly seen from chapter eight onwards when the testimony is no longer to the Jew alone but extends to Samaria and the nations in general. Nonetheless, we will see that the testimony is always "to Jew first" (Rom. 1: 16). Thus, we will now have a mixed character of things and connections will no longer be so clear as previously. Hence the paramount importance of maintaining the links previously proved in the Gospels and in the earlier section of the Acts, namely, ***that miracles as signs are identified with the Jew alone and have no particular significance to the Gentile***. It follows that we will continue to have miracles as signs, but not with the same focus and frequency that existed when the testimony was restricted to Jerusalem. Thus, miracles continue, with those performed by Paul being every bit as distinctive as those performed by Peter, ***but not with the abundance as when the testimony was restricted to Jerusalem***.[12] The Gentiles also benefit from them, but their significance is reduced, and we never read of the word *sign* after chapter 15. Not without significance, this is also the last time that we read of Peter in the Acts. However, the testimony is still of the Kingdom of God throughout and we hear ***nothing of the truth of the Mystery***. Indeed, throughout Acts Christianity is not viewed as distinct but as a sect of Judaism (as we shall see later). Initially, Peter is dominant in the testimony, but, as just

---

[12] In keeping with this, the word *sign(s)* in the sense of miracle(s) occurs nine times in the record of the testimony in Jerusalem but only four times after the testimony has left that city. Two of these four occurrences are in connection with the testimony in Samaria (see Acts 8: 6, 13), while the other two occurrences are not relative to particular signs but are only general statements (see Acts 14: 3; 15: 12).

mentioned, after Acts 15 we hear nothing more of Peter and the twelve, and Paul becomes the leading vessel in the testimony.

Again, while judgment is soon to fall on Jerusalem and the Jew, God in mercy delays that moment until finally enacted by Titus in AD 70 some ten or more years after the history of the Acts closed. There is thus a parallel with the glory of Jehovah departing in the book of Ezekiel. Then it was not an immediate or sudden departure, but a gradual withdrawal. Nonetheless the glory eventually did go. In Ez. 9: 3; 10: 4 we read of its departure from the cherub (above the ark in the temple), then in Ez. 10: 18 from over the threshold of the house of Jehovah, then from the east gate of the house in v19 and finally from the midst of the city in Ez. 11: 23. God likewise lingered with Israel in the time of the Acts, firstly after the crucifixion of Christ, then after the stoning of Stephen in Jerusalem and finally with the rejection of Paul's testimony to the dispersion in Acts 28. Nonetheless, as Paul warned in his epistle to the Romans (written, as regards time, towards the end of the book of Acts) Israel would be set aside in judgment and the Gentiles would become the focus of blessing.

**The Advent of the Testimony to the Gentiles**

In keeping with the Lord's word "and ye shall be my witnesses both in Jerusalem, and in all Judaea and Samaria, and to the end of the earth" (Acts 1: 8) we find that, initially, occasioned by the stoning of Stephen, "all were scattered into the countries of Judaea and Samaria except the apostles ... Those then that had been scattered went through [the countries] announcing the glad tidings of the word" (Acts 8: 1-4). Now we must carefully consider the testimony in Samaria for it bears heavily on what I have said concerning signs and raises a number of questions that I must attempt to answer.

The Lord directed that once the testimony left Jerusalem, it would go firstly to Judaea and Samaria before eventually going to the end of the earth. Judaea, the country of the Jews, we can well understand, but why Samaria and the Samaritans? Why are the Samaritans and Samaria singled out in this specific way, for they were not Jews? We read "And Philip, going down to a city of Samaria, preached the Christ to them" (Acts 8: 5). Why was Philip, a Hellenist and not one of the twelve indigenous Jewish apostles, given this service? We further read that:

> … the crowds with one accord gave heed to the things spoken by Philip, when they heard [him] and saw the signs which he wrought. For from many who had unclean spirits they went out, crying with a loud voice; and many that were paralysed and lame were healed. (vs. 6, 7).

His testimony likewise involved "announcing the glad tidings concerning the kingdom of God and the name of Jesus Christ" (v12) and was confirmed by "the signs and great works of power which took place" (v13). If the signs were for the Jews, why did God give signs to the Samaritans? However, we also read:

> And the apostles … sent to them Peter and John; who, having come down, prayed for them that they might receive [the] Holy Spirit; for he was not yet fallen upon any of them, only they were baptised to the name of the Lord Jesus. Then they laid their hands upon them, and they received [the] Holy Spirit. (vs. 14–17).

Why did the Samaritans not receive the Holy Spirit until Peter and John laid hands upon them? Now the Samaritans were certainly not Jews, nor were they quite just Gentiles either. Samaria had been populated by the ten tribes (see 2 Kings 17: 1, 2). When these had been taken into captivity by Assyria (see v6), the country was inhabited by a mixed population (see v 24) —a mongrel nation with a mixed religion (see vs. 25-41). Yet the Samaritans claimed to be of Israel for the Samaritan woman at Sychar's well spoke of "our father Jacob" (John 4: 12) and, at one time, they had a rival temple to that in Jerusalem for she said, "Our fathers worshipped in this mountain" (v20). Indeed, like the Jews of Judaea she knew "that Messias is coming, who is called Christ" (v25). Thus, the Samaritans claimed to be the chosen people, but the claim was false for, as the Lord told the Samaritan woman, "salvation is of the Jews" (v22). Whether any among them could trace their ancestry back to the ten tribes is open to question, but, like the woman, there were those among them who wrongly thought that their claim was true. However, God's Word was now "the word of his grace" (Acts 14: 3). Thus, if in God's wondrous grace the testimony began at Jerusalem, the very city outside whose walls the Christ had been crucified, then in a further flow of that grace God would confirm His Word with signs to those who made a claim (even though it was false) on Israel's King. Hence God through Philip gave signs to the Samaritans. However, note it well, ***these are the last specific signs recorded in Acts*** although the word *sign* is used in a general sense twice more in Acts 14: 3 and 15: 12. ***There are no recorded signs ever given to Gentiles in Acts***.[13]

But why was it Philip that took the testimony into Samaria? As already stated, Philip, was a Hellenist and one of the seven (see Acts 21: 8)—that is, he was not an apostle. Now the animosity between Judaea and Samaria was proverbial and the Samaritan woman's word "Jews have no intercourse with Samaritans" (John 4: 9) was really an understatement. Hence it was more agreeable for the testimony to be taken to Samaria by a Hellenist, with a Greek name (Philip), than by a native of Judaea. Nonetheless, while God thus acted in marvellous grace, He would not allow Samaria to claim equality with Jerusalem and He would not allow the ancient rivalry to continue by giving the gift of the Holy Spirit independently of the apostles at Jerusalem. There was to be one Church. Accordingly it is only when that identification takes place with the laying on of the hands of Peter and John that the Samaritans "received [the] Holy Spirit" (Acts 8: 17).

After these things, Peter's service continues in Judaea, and at Lydda Aeneas is healed with the words "Aeneas, Jesus, the Christ, heals thee" (Acts 9: 34) followed by the resurrection of Dorcas, with the result that "many believed on the Lord" (v 42). Chapters 10 and 11 see Peter using the keys of the Kingdom which had been given to him by the Lord (see Matt. 16: 19) to provide entrance to Cornelius, the first of the Gentiles. Here we have the second stated occasion in the book of the exercise of tongues. As already shown, this was not to confirm the faith of Cornelius and his household but to testify to the Jews present that the Gentiles had received the Holy Spirit: "for they heard them speaking with tongues and magnifying God" (Acts 10: 46). We then read the words "Then Peter answered" so that a question, vocally or implied, must have been raised to which an answer must be given. The answer given is that the gift of tongues to the Gentiles was a clear sign for the Jews present that the Gentiles had received the Holy Spirit: "Then

---

[13] The miracles by Paul on the island of Melita (Malta) as recorded in Acts 28: 3–10 are never said to be signs. They were miracles performed for the benefit of Gentiles and not in the presence of Jews.

Peter answered, Can any one forbid water that these should not be baptised, who have received the Holy Spirit as we also [did]?" (v47). Thus, the testimony which was first given to the Jew is now given to the Gentile as well. This order of Jew then Gentile is preserved throughout the history of the Acts—as we will see in a moment after we have looked at the apostolic nature of the testimony of signs.

**The Apostolic Nature of the Testimonial Exercise of Signs**

After the Gentile was introduced into blessing in the person of Cornelius, the public testimony as recorded in Acts largely rests with the Apostle Paul whose conversion is recorded in Acts 9. Ananias is told by the Lord that "this [man] is an elect vessel to me, to bear my name before both nations and kings and [the] sons of Israel" (Acts 9: 15). This Scripture puts the Gentiles ***before*** the Jews, ***showing that there was going to be a radical change in the ways of God***—but this will not take place, as we will see, until the history of Acts has run its course.

Now while Paul testifies immediately after his conversion at Damascus (see Acts 9: 19, 20) and Jerusalem (see vs. 28. 29), there is no record that he performed any miracles or signs in those places (indeed, after the stoning of Stephen, ***there is no record that Jerusalem ever witnessed a miracle again***). It is only after the Holy Spirit said "Separate me now Barnabas and Saul for the work to which I have called them ... They therefore, having been sent forth by the Holy Spirit ..." (Acts 13: 2, 4)—that is, when they were divinely and publicly appointed as apostles—that we read of the first miracle at the hands of Paul (see vs. 6–12). There is no miracle from the hands of Paul or Barnabas until their apostleship is confirmed by the Holy Spirit and it is only subsequently that they are referred to as apostles (see Acts 14: 4).

Now Paul later speaks of those "who were in surpassing degree apostles" (2 Cor. 12: 11) and then goes on to say to the Corinthians that the "The signs indeed of the apostle were wrought among you in all endurance, signs, and wonders, and works of power" (v 12). The sense here cannot be that while signs belonged to believers generally, there were certain peculiar signs that belonged to the apostles alone. Why? Because when Paul expands on the use of the word *signs* in v12, he does not do this by listing specific signs peculiar to the apostles ***but by using the very same triple designation that is used in the book of***

***Hebrews*** that describes the means that God employed to confirm the testimony of those that heard (see Heb. 2 vs. 3, 4): "signs and wonders, and various acts of power" (v 4). The sense is thus not that some signs were distinctive to the apostles but rather that the ***signs belonged to the apostles alone***. This is in line with what has already been said regarding Mark 16 and the fact that Paul and Barnabas performed no signs until they were commissioned as apostles by the Holy Spirit. While the testimony was restricted to Jerusalem we read that "many wonders and signs took place through the apostles' means" (Acts 2: 43) and again, we read that "with great power did the apostles give witness of the resurrection of the Lord Jesus" (Acts 4: 33) and "by the hands of the apostles were many signs[14] and wonders done among the people" (Acts 5: 12).

When the testimony left Jerusalem, it was taken by those who were scattered after the stoning of Stephen and who then announced "the glad tidings of the word" (Acts 8: 4) ***but there is no record that these believers performed a single sign***. These believers are again referred to later as speaking "to the Greeks also, announcing the glad tidings of the Lord Jesus" (Acts 11: 20) and we read in the following verse of conversions resulting from their testimony, ***but we do not read of any accompanying miracles***. While this is negative, it nonetheless lends weight to what has already been said, namely that the signs were peculiar to the apostles. ***There is no record of any sign taking place unless by the twelve apostles (two of whom are named—Peter and John), the apostles Paul and Barnabas, and Stephen and Philip (who, like the rest of the seven, were identified with the apostles by the laying on of hands).***

However, there is little doubt that within the assembly believers exercised gifts and some may have performed miracles (but not signs) as the words "He therefore who ministers to you the Spirit, and works miracles among you ..." (Gal. 3: 5) although abstract, seem to indicate. Nonetheless the miracles performed are not said to be signs. ***Again, I stress that there is certainly no record in Scripture that signs were performed by believers in general***.

---

[14] Notice that the word in these Scriptures is "signs" not "miracles"—that is, we are to appreciate that although these clearly were miracles, they had significance and hence were fraught with meaning.

## To the Jew First

While the Gentile had now been brought into blessing in the person of Cornelius, the repentant Jew was blessed first and this principle, set down by the apostle as "both to Jew first and to Greek" (Rom. 1: 16) is adhered to throughout the rest of the Acts (which is largely within the ministry of Paul). In Salamis, Barnabas and Paul "announced the word of God in the synagogues of the Jews" (Acts 13: 5). The same pattern of going to the synagogues of the Jews first is followed consistently in Antioch of Pisidia, in Iconium, in Thessalonica, in Berea, in Athens, in Corinth and in Ephesus (see Acts 13: 14; 14: 1; 17: 1, 10, 16, 17; 18: 1-4, 19; 19: 8). This approach we are told was "according to Paul's custom" (Acts 17: 2). Even when there was no synagogue in a place (such as at Philippi) they sought their own people first and "went outside the gate by the river, where it was the custom for prayer to be" (Acts 16: 13). Again, when Jew and Gentile (or Greek) are spoken of, the Jew is always[15] put first (as in Acts 14:1; 18: 4, 19: 10, 17; 20: 21; 26: 23). At Antioch it is only when Paul's testimony to the Jews and their proselytes was rejected that Paul says to them "lo, we turn to the nations" (Acts 13: 46) but this was local, not universal, for again and again he resorts to the Jews first. At Corinth he again says, "from henceforth I will go to the nations" (Acts 18: 6). Again, this was only local for in Ephesus after encountering the disciples of John he goes first to the synagogue (see Acts 19: 8) and only on the rejection of his testimony does he go to the school of Tyrannus—a Gentile location. At the very end of the book when Paul arrives at Rome who does he first call to him? The leaders of the Church? No, but "the chief of the Jews" (Acts 28: 17). ***Hence throughout the whole of the book of Acts, the Jew has priority in the testimony***.

## The Miracles of Paul

In regard to the miracles performed by the apostles, it is a striking fact in the record of Scripture that Peter and the twelve performed no miracle outside of Judaea and that Paul performed no miracles in

[15] With the exception of Acts 9: 15, already alluded to.

Judaea.[16] Indeed, as already mentioned, while Paul testified immediately after his conversion at Damascus (see Acts 9: 20) and Jerusalem (see v28), there is no record that he performed any miracles in those places. His first recorded miracle only took place after he was called by the Holy Spirit to be an apostle (see Acts 13: 2–4) and that was to render a Jewish false prophet sightless for a season because he hindered the testimony to an enquiring Gentile (see vs. 6–12). Later we have the general statement "They stayed therefore a good while, speaking boldly, [confiding] in the Lord, who gave witness to the word of his grace, giving signs and wonders to be done by their hands" (Acts 14: 3), which, as the following verse shows, was clearly in the presence of Jews. The healing of the man impotent on his feet at Lystra (see vs. 8–20), done in the presence of Gentiles, is not said to be a sign. Thus miracles, that serve as signs to Jews, are no longer limited to Jews.

At the council in Jerusalem, we read that "all the multitude kept silence and listened to Barnabas and Paul relating all the signs and wonders which God had wrought among[17] the nations by them" (Acts 15: 12). In Philippi Paul removes the spirit of Python (see Acts 16: 16–18) from the possessed woman and in Acts 19: 6 we have the former disciples of the Baptist speaking with tongues and prophesying after Paul has laid his hands on them. In the latter incident, the words "And entering into the synagogue ..." (v8) show, as already pointed out, that this incident took place close to the synagogue and in the presence of Jews. In the same chapter we are also told of the power exercised by Paul: "And God wrought no ordinary miracles by the hands of Paul, so that even napkins or aprons were brought from his body [and put] upon the sick, and the diseases left them, and the wicked spirits went out" (vs. 11, 12). As for the incident of Acts 20: 9–12, it is questionable if this was a miracle. Lastly, the healing of the father of Publius and the subsequent healing of the sick on Melita (see Acts 28: 7–10) are not spoken of as signs to the Jews—for Scripture does not record that there were any present—but the exercise of the Apostle's gift of healing to the Gentiles.

---

[16] For the difference between the ministries of Peter and Paul was, as Paul says, "that the glad tidings of the uncircumcision were confided to me, even as to Peter that of the circumcision" (Gal. 2: 7).

[17] The word among in Greek is *en* which simply locates where the signs took place and does not necessarily suggest that the nations were the object of those signs. The same Greek phrase *en tois ethnesin* is used in 1 Pet. 2: 12 where the sense is also one of location as clearly seen by the context.

## The Absence of the Mystery in the Book of Acts

The subject in the book of Acts from beginning to end is the Kingdom of God. The one ***unique*** feature of Christianity, namely the Mystery, is entirely absent. It is true that both Jew and Gentile had the same Gospel preached to them, and that the response to that Gospel had to be the same in both cases, but nonetheless, once blessed, the distinctions between them were not entirely set aside in the period covered by Acts. There is nothing at all of the unity of Jew and Gentile in one body, ***with all previous barriers broken down and united to a glorified Christ in heaven***. This truth is the teaching of the later prison epistles, Ephesians and Colossians. The Church is there in Acts, but its distinctive constitution is as yet unknown.

However, it may be objected that the Lord's words to Paul "*I* am Jesus, whom *thou* persecutest" (Acts 9: 5) embrace the truth of the Mystery. This is true ***but only with the full knowledge of the prison epistles that allows us to interpret them in that way***. Again, the fact that the Lord identified Himself with His persecuted saints on earth is certainly not peculiar to the Church (see Matt. 25: 34–40). Until Acts 10[18] there is not a single Gentile in the Church, and from Acts 10 to 28, the Jew always has priority and is viewed as distinct. There is no teaching in the book of Acts that is not in the OT or the Gospels. If the entrance of the Gentiles into blessing, foretold in the OT, caused a stir among the Jewish believers (see Acts 11: 3; 15: 1), what would the statement as to Christ having "broken down the middle wall of enclosure ... that he might form the two in himself into one new man" (Eph. 2: 14, 15) have done? But those words were written years after the period covered by the Acts had closed, and after the testimony of the Kingdom of God had been finally rejected by the dispersion (see Acts 28: 25–28). That peculiar truth of Christianity, the Mystery, was not made known in the OT, or in the Gospels, or to previous generations (see Rom. 16: 25; Eph. 3: 5; Col. 1: 26), but was revealed to Paul (see Eph. 3: 3) and by the Lord to "his holy apostles and prophets" (v5) and "has now been made manifest" (not revealed) "to his saints" (Col. 1: 26). While that knowledge may have been made known to ***some*** in the time span of the Acts, it did not form part of the ***public*** teaching for Paul speaks of himself as:

[18] The context of Acts 8: 27–40 shows that the Ethiopian was either a Jew or a proselyte.

> … witnessing both to small and great, saying ***nothing else than those things which both the prophets and Moses have said should happen***, [namely,] whether Christ should suffer; whether he first, through resurrection of [the] dead, should announce light both to the people and to the nations.
> (Acts 26: 22, 23—my emphasis).

If Paul had publicly declared that the middle wall of enclosure had been broken down, he could not have said at the end of Acts that he had "done nothing against the people ***or the customs of our forefathers***" (Acts 28: 17—my emphasis). If, in the time span of the Acts, Paul had said nothing that was not in the OT, and as the Mystery was not in the OT, then He had not taught the Mystery publicly. How different this is to Eph. 3: 9 where Paul wants "to enlighten all [with the knowledge of] what is the administration of the mystery"! What was taught in the Acts was in the OT and the Gospels. It was the "***beginning*** of the Christ" (Heb. 6: 1—my emphasis) not the end! Though ***essential***, it was ***initial***. It belonged to childhood, not manhood (see Heb. 5: 12–14). Thus in Heb. 6: 1, the writer exhorts the Jewish believers to leave the beginning of the Christ and to go on to what belonged to ***full growth***—maturity. Six things are given which are the beginning of the Christ and every one of them is found in the OT or the Gospels ***and in the book of Acts***:

1. Wherefore, leaving the word of the beginning of the Christ, let us go on [to what belongs] to full growth, not laying again a foundation of repentance from dead works (see Acts 2: 38; 3: 19; 8: 22; 17: 30; 26: 20)
2. and faith in God (see Acts 3: 16; 10: 43)
3. of [the] doctrine of washings, (baptisms—same word, see Acts 2: 38; 22: 16)
4. and of imposition of hands (see Acts 8: 17; 13: 3; 19: 6)
5. and of resurrection of [the] dead (see Acts 17: 31; 23: 6; 26: 23)
6. and of eternal judgment (see Acts 17: 31; 24: 25)

The truth of the Mystery, so necessary for full growth (see Eph. 4: 13), is absent in Acts and Hebrews.

**Sects and The Way**

Now in keeping with the absence of the Mystery in Acts, we find that Christianity as seen by men was nothing more than another sect of the Jews, no different in that respect to the Sadducees and the Pharisees (see Acts 5: 17 and 15: 5 respectively). In Rome the leaders of the dispersion speak of Christianity saying, "as concerning this sect it is known to us that it is everywhere spoken against" (Acts 28: 22) and Tertullus describes Paul as "a leader of the sect of the Nazaraeans" (Acts 24: 5). Clearly, as far as men were concerned, Christianity was just another sect of Judaism.

While the expression *the way* is clearly used in a general sense in the Gospels and elsewhere, it is employed in a distinctive and peculiar manner in the book of Acts to describe Christianity in its early days (see Acts 9: 2; 19: 9, 23; 22: 4; 24: 14, 22). Outside the Acts, it is not used in that manner except possibly in Mark 10: 32, 52. Now Paul in replying to Tertullus, does not deny his assertion that Christianity was a sect of Judaism, but instead says "But this I avow to thee, that in the way which they call sect, so I serve my fathers' God" (Acts 24: 14). While the Apostle does not accept Christianity as ***just another*** sect of Judaism like the Pharisees and the Sadducees (and thus at best their peer) ***he does not in his reply divorce Christianity from Judaism***. The words "so I serve my fathers' God" clearly link Christianity with the past. When we read of Paul's past, he says that he had "persecuted this way unto death" (Acts 22: 4) and the Christians that he persecuted were clearly all Jews (see also Acts 9: 2)—for at that time there was not a single Gentile in the Church. ***Hence the term 'the way' refers to Christianity as a pathway within Judaism, not separate from it or out of it***. It is only later that Paul speaks of "Jews, or Greeks, or the assembly of God" (1 Cor. 10: 32).

However, some may object that if Paul had not taught the truth of the Mystery in the period of the Acts, how could he claim to the elders at Ephesus that he had not "shrunk from announcing to you all the counsel of God" (Acts 20: 27), as surely ***all*** the counsel of God must include the Mystery? While not wishing to weaken the embracive force of the word "all", we must not extract the words from the context. In v25 he had spoken of "preaching the kingdom [of God]" and hence the word "all" is limited to the divine counsel regarding the Kingdom and we have no warrant in extending the word "all" beyond the Kingdom.[19]

Lastly, in this regard it would be difficult, if not impossible, to argue intelligently that the equality of Jew and Gentile in one body could be rightly understood when Paul acquiesced to the distinction that James maintains between Jew and Gentile as recorded in Acts 21: 25 (in the sense that the Jews were to continue in the Mosaic law, with the Gentiles subject to lesser restrictions). Clearly at that point in time the barriers between them in the Church had not been finally broken down and would not be until Israel was finally set aside in judgment.

**Summary**

I have sought to establish the following points from the Scriptures:

- The signs continued during this period but not with the multiplicity that existed when the testimony was restricted to Jerusalem
- God in grace gave signs to the Samaritans, even though their claims were false, but they only received the Holy Spirit through the hands of Jewish apostles
- The signs were always given by apostles (or by those identified with them by the laying on of hands)
- Throughout Acts the testimony always went to the Jew first
- Again, throughout Acts there is no public testimony to the Mystery
- Accordingly Christianity is not as yet divorced from Judaism

---

19 In a similar way the word "all" is not absolute in "for all have sinned" (Rom. 3: 23)—for there are angels that have not sinned. The context makes it clear that only men are in view. Similarly, the context of Acts 20 makes it plain that the word "all" must be understood in relation to the counsel concerning the Kingdom of God.

# Chapter 7

# The Mystery and the Cessation of the Signs

## Introduction

The exact dates of any of the epistles cannot be given with any certainty. However, without doubt, the epistles to the Romans, Corinthians, Galatians, Thessalonians, and that of James were written within the period of the Acts.[20] Although some doubt it, there is good evidence that Hebrews was also written around this time. Strikingly, the epistles written within this period are the ***only epistles in which we read of signs***. Signs are not mentioned in any epistle written after the history of the Acts closed.

Now while the concept of the one body is taught by Paul in both Romans and 1 Corinthians, the point of the apostle's teaching in these epistles is not the unity of Jew and Gentile, nor the equality in the body of all believers. The truth of the body is introduced in relation to the gifts. Not all the gifts are equal (see 1 Cor. 12: 31) but although they are distinctive, their object is one, namely the building up of the Church as the body of Christ, not the exaltation of those who possess them. Again, there is no thought in the contents of these epistles of the Church being united by the Holy Spirit to the Head in heaven—the ***full*** thought of the Mystery. The closing verses of Romans (Rom. 16: 25–27) which briefly refer to the Mystery without any development are considered by many to be an appendix[21] and their

---

[20] This is the virtually universal view of all authorities on the subject. It is also substantiated by the internal evidence of the epistles themselves. For example, it is clear that Paul arrived in Rome for the first time in Acts 28: 16. Yet when he wrote Rom. 1: 13–15; 15: 22–24 he had not, as yet, been there. Hence Romans was obviously written before the history of the Acts had closed.

[21] The last three verses of Rom. 16 form a doxology but are peculiar in that they occupy different positions in the various Greek manuscripts of the Roman epistle. Now the normal ending of an epistle is a benediction, not a doxology, with such words as "The grace of the Lord Jesus Christ ..." (1 Cor. 16: 23)—not a note of praise (a doxology). Even when we have both a doxology and a benediction in an epistle, the benediction comes after the doxology (see Phil. 4: 20, 23; 1 Tim. 6: 15, 16, 21 and 2 Tim. 4: 18, 22). In Rom. 16 we have the benedictions in vs. 20 and 24 followed by the doxology of vs. 25–27. Many scholars have noted this, and the only consistent response

setting indicates that these verses were added later by the apostle—possibly after the history of the Acts had closed. Now the most important epistle within the time frame of the Acts regarding the continuation of miracles is the first Corinthian epistle. However, before we turn to that letter, we must note the distinction between signs and gifts.

### The Distinction between Signs and Gifts

I said earlier that there is a distinction between signs and gifts. Some signs are also gifts (healing and tongues), some signs (exorcism and the taking up of serpents) are never said to be gifts, and again some gifts (teaching and helps) are never said to be signs. As already shown, the signs belong to the Kingdom and are for the Jew and were ***always given by Jews***; the gifts belong to the Church and are thus for all men irrespective of nationality.

Clearly a sign is an unusual happening pointing to something or someone and is commonly a miracle. There are plenty of signs in the OT, of which the ones mentioned most were those performed in Egypt when God took up Israel as a nation. In the Gospels, as already shown, the miracles were generally signs identifying Jesus as the Messiah to the Jews and indicating that the time had come for the Kingdom to be set up in power on earth. Thus, signs belong to the Kingdom and not the Church.

What is a gift? The Bible employs terms used in the natural realm to express things in the spiritual realm. Thus, Christ and the Church are figured by the Head and the body respectively because the natural head and its relationship to the natural body are clearly understood. Likewise, we know what is meant by a gifted pianist. It does not mean one who can play the piano but one whose playing is distinctive and outstanding. The same is true with the spiritual gifts. A man used for the conversion of others is not necessarily an evangelist. Those scattered abroad after the stoning of Stephen were evangelical and got conversions (see Acts 11: 19–21) but it is Philip who is singled out and called "the evangelist" (Acts 21: 8), for the Spirit of God records his outstanding and distinctive service in Samaria to "the crowds" (Acts 8: 6), in Gaza to the individual (see v27) and elsewhere (see v40).

---

is that the position of vs. 25–27 in the English Bible is the correct one and that Paul added these words later after the rest of the epistle was in general circulation.

An evangelist is one who gets outstanding results with his labours in the Gospel.

But what are the gifts for? They are for the Church. When the Lord was on earth, the Church did not exist for the Lord had said "...I ***will*** build my assembly" (Matt. 16: 18—my emphasis). The gifts were given consequent on His ascension: "Having ascended up on high, he ... has given gifts to men" (Eph. 4: 8) and they are for the body of Christ: "he has given some apostles ... with a view to the edifying of the body of Christ" (vs. 11, 12). Thus, the gifts belong to the Church.

What was the purpose of the gifts? In Ephesians we read that the Lord:

> ... has given some apostles, and some prophets, and some evangelists, and some shepherds and teachers, for the perfecting of the saints; with a view to [the] work of [the] ministry, with a view to the edifying of the body of Christ. (Eph. 4: 11, 12).

In a similar vein in Corinthians, we are told that "to each the manifestation of the Spirit is given for profit" (1 Cor. 12: 7), and in relation to the gifts and to tongues in particular, Paul says "seek that ye may abound for the edification of the assembly" (1 Cor. 14: 12). The purpose of the gifts was therefore for the edification (that is, the spiritual building up) of the Church.

Now we read of the gifts[22] in the epistles written during the time span of the Acts (Corinthians, Romans and James) and in those written after the history of that book has closed (Ephesians and Timothy), but we only read of the signs in the epistles written within the period of the Acts (Romans, Corinthians, Thessalonians and Hebrews) and ***never after***.

Exorcism is a sign (Mark 16: 17) but is never called a gift, for demon–possessed men are clearly not in the Church but are under the control of the Devil. The casting out of demons has nothing to do with the building up of the Church. Likewise, teaching is a gift and is never

---

22 There are some 20 distinct gifts spoken of in Romans, 1 Corinthians and Ephesians. In Rom. 12: 6–9 we have prophecy, service, teaching, exhortation, giving, leading and showing mercy; in 1 Cor. 12: 8–10, 28–30 we have the word of wisdom, the word of knowledge, faith, gifts of healing, operations of miracles, prophecy, discerning of spirits, kinds of tongues, interpretation of tongues, apostles, teachers, helps and governments; in Eph. 4: 11 we have apostles, prophets, evangelists, shepherds and teachers.

called a sign—for teaching, in itself, has no distinctive significance. But why are some signs such as healing and tongues also classed as gifts? Because of the transitional state of things in the book of Acts in which the testimony of the Kingdom to the Jew continued (corroborated by the signs) while the Church (in which the same miracles were exercised as gifts) was being set up. Once the Jew was set aside, the signs ceased and those gifts which were also signs stopped as well. In the local assembly the public use of tongues, without interpretation, was forbidden by Paul because "He that speaks with a tongue edifies himself" (1 Cor. 14: 4) and not the assembly. Without interpretation, tongues had no value in the assembly. In themselves miracles, healings and tongues contribute nothing spiritually to the "perfecting of the saints ... the edifying of the body of Christ" (Eph. 4: 12). Hence, as we shall see, once the Jew is set aside nationally, these sign–gifts and certain others will cease.

**The Thirteenth Chapter of 1 Corinthians**

The first epistle to the Corinthians contains a wealth of information about the gifts and it is in chapter 13 that we are told that there is to be a cessation of certain signs and gifts. This is a key Scripture for our subject and its correct interpretation is vital.

In regard to the cessation of certain gifts, we read that "when that which is perfect has come, that which is in part shall be done away" (1 Cor. 13: 10). Clearly from this chapter "when that which is perfect has come" then certain gifts will cease. The fulcrum on which everything pivots is the meaning of "that which is perfect". While there is general agreement that the gifts spoken of in 1 Cor. 13: 8–13 will end, the disagreement is ***when*** they end. The majority view is that "that which is perfect" refers to the completion of the Church when ***all*** the gifts will no longer be needed and the parallel is drawn between 1 Cor. 13 and Eph. 4: 10–13 to substantiate this idea. However, while this view may appear to be correct, on close examination it is seen to be erroneous.[23]

A gift, a "manifestation of the Spirit is given for profit" (1 Cor. 12: 7) and for edification (see 1 Cor. 14: 3–5). The gifts were not all equal, for the Corinthians were to "desire earnestly the greater gifts" (1 Cor. 12: 31) of which prophecy was one (see 1 Cor. 14: 1). Now ***in contrast*** to

---

[23] See Appendix 2.

even the greater gifts, Paul says “yet show I unto you a way of more surpassing excellence” (1 Cor. 12: 31). A way for what? For building up the Church and that way is love.[24] Without it all else is valueless. Even prophecy, one of the greater gifts, is but temporal; but love abides and is eternal. Thus, Paul says of the body that it “works for itself the increase of the body to its self–building up in love” (Eph. 4: 16).

In contrast to love we are told “but whether prophecies, they shall be done away; or tongues, they shall cease; or knowledge, it shall be done away” (1 Cor. 13: 8). Now prophecies and tongues are both signs and gifts, but what about knowledge? This cannot be knowledge in the general sense for Paul goes on to say, “but ***then*** I shall know according as I also have been known” (v12, my emphasis). In verse 2 knowledge is linked with prophecy, mysteries, and faith. In 1 Cor. 12: 8–10, along with the gifts of faith and prophecy, we have the “word of knowledge” (v8). Thus prophecy, tongues and knowledge are all gifts. Why does the apostle single these three out as those that are going to cease? What is the link between them? ***They all have to do with the Word of God***, whereas healing, for example, does not. Prophecy and the word of knowledge ***directly*** gave the mind of God[25] and tongues did so ***indirectly*** through one who could interpret (see 1 Cor. 14: 2–8). The use of such gifts in an assembly are for the edification of the Church as Paul says in 1 Cor. 14: 1–14. Prophesy (see v3), knowledge (see v6) and tongues with interpretation (see v13) are all mentioned.[26] We must remember that when Paul wrote to Corinth, the NT was far from complete. Again, Israel was not, as yet, judicially set aside and so the establishment of the Kingdom in power was still a distinct possibility consequent on that nation’s repentance. The Mystery, the unique characteristic of the Church was not generally known. Thus, the mind of God for the moment could only be made known through these gifts, that is mainly prophecy and knowledge. What is “that which is perfect”

---

[24] Hence, even in the absence of gifts in a local assembly, the exercise of love will ensure the building up of the Church.

[25] Perusal of the use of prophecy in both the OT and the NT shows that it was the revelation of the mind of God to certain persons regarding particular circumstances. The foretelling of the future in prophecy was secondary. The word of knowledge would be the revelation of some aspect of the truth as yet not in the Scriptures.

[26] The fact that the gift of tongues requires interpretation to be of value in expressing the mind of God may be the reason that Paul drops it from his argument in 1 Cor. 13: 9. Again, you will notice that while prophecy and knowledge are said to be “done away” (v8) or ‘put an end to’, tongues are simply said to “cease”(v8)—a bald statement whereas the other two are subject to a positive action.

(1 Cor. 13: 10) then? It can only be knowledge. For these gifts which are "in part" (v9) alone allow one to say, "now I know partially" (v12) but "when that which is perfect" (or *complete*—the same Greek word) "has come, that which is in part" (the gifts named) "shall be done away" (v10). When knowledge is complete, the means of communicating knowledge in part will be done away. An example may illustrate this. A renowned author completes his latest book. Before publication, a national newspaper publishes extracts from the book. Avid followers of the author will purchase the newspaper to read the extracts. Those who have friends who are unable to do so will keep the relevant copies of the newspaper for them. When the book is finally published, the eager readers will buy copies of the book. What will happen to the newspaper copies so eagerly read a short while ago? They will be discarded. Why? Because when that which is complete (in this example, the book) is come, that which is in part (in this example, the newspaper extracts) will be done away.

We must now look at the two illustrations that Paul gives in 1 Cor. 13: 11, 12. The first compares a child[27] with a man. There is no difference in nature or substance between the two, only maturity or growth. The child is not imperfect in the sense of having some deformity but only in the sense of being immature. Now in v11 the apostle details three things in relation to the child which may be paralleled with the three gifts: "spoke" (tongues), "felt" (prophecy), "reasoned" (knowledge). The thinking, the reasoning, and the ability to express oneself are all limited in the case of the child. Likewise, these gifts were suited to the initial immature state of the Church but when the mind of God was fully expressed by the revelation of the truth of the Mystery they were done away, just as the mature man discards that which belongs to childhood.

The second illustration for "now" and "then" is of an incomplete, imperfect or partial view through some medium such as a window or mirror (again, the illustration is carefully chosen—for Corinth was famous for its brass mirrors). The image is obscure, blurred and the

---

[27] Strictly, a babe—one who cannot speak properly—a fact that would not be lost on the Corinthians who were boastful of their gift of tongues. By inference Paul is telling them that they are just babes that cannot talk properly! Incidentally, this word for babes is one that Paul always appears to use in contrast with manhood in a deprecatory manner.

resolution poor. The word used for *obscurely*[28] is the Greek word from which we get our word *enigmatically*. There is that in the image which puzzles the viewer as not all the details are clear and hence the knowledge is incomplete. Another would see him as he is, not as he has to view himself through the imperfect medium of a mirror. Because of the mirror's poor resolution, a man's knowledge of his face would be incomplete. It refers to the Corinthian's present knowledge. In contrast, when the Mystery is revealed "then I shall know according as I also have been known" (1 Cor. 13: 12). This does not mean that infinite knowledge (omniscience) would be possessed for that belongs to God alone. The sense is not the ***amount*** of knowledge, but the ***completeness*** of that knowledge, for there is no ground whatsoever to take the words "I shall know according as I also have been known" to assume that this refers to God's knowledge of me. The clause is simply indefinite and abstract. The sense is that I shall see myself as another (whoever he may be) sees me; I shall know myself as another (whoever he may be) knows me. The knowledge is finite but complete.

However, the full knowledge that initiates the putting away of the gifts of prophecy and knowledge is the Mystery, for this completes the Word of God. Paul speaks of "the dispensation of God which [is] given me towards you to complete the word of God" (Col. 1: 25). Now this cannot mean that Paul thought that he was the last of the inspired NT writers for the word used for *complete* is not *teleioo*, which has the sense of *to bring to a full end* and would have been used if the writer had wished to convey that his writings were the last. The word used is *pleroo* which carries the sense of *to fill up*. Putting v25 in context, the sense is clear, for Paul speaks in the previous verse of Christ's body, the Church,

> ... of which *I* became minister, according to the dispensation of God which [is] given me towards you to complete the word of God, the mystery which [has been] hidden from ages and from generations, but has now been made manifest to his saints.
> (vs. 25, 26).

---

[28] We have a similar example in Num. 12: 8 where the same word is used in the Greek Septuagint and is translated "riddles". Jehovah spoke to Moses mouth to mouth, not in riddles (that is obscurely) or through a prophet (see Num. 12: 6).

It is what Paul calls "the mystery" that completes, fills up, "the word of God" (v25). Hence it is a question of ***content*** not of ***time***. In regard to time, John probably wrote later; in regard to content, there is nothing new in John's ***subject*** matter that is not found elsewhere in the Bible. In Scripture, the subject of the Mystery is peculiar to Paul. This Mystery or secret (the Greek word for *mystery, musterion*,[29] means something only known to the initiated) was hidden in past ages (see Rom. 16: 25; Eph. 3: 9; Col. 1: 26) from previous generations (see Eph. 3: 5; Col 1: 26) but was made known firstly to Paul (see Eph. 3: 3), then to Christ's "holy apostles and prophets" (v5), recorded in "prophetic scriptures" (Rom. 16: 26) and finally manifested "to his saints" (Col. 1: 26). Thus, there could be nothing of this Mystery in the OT. What then is this secret?

## The Mystery

In almost the whole of the OT God dealt with Israel alone. In the Gospels the Lord said that "I have not been sent save to the lost sheep of Israel's house" (Matt. 15: 24). In the early history of the Church in Acts the testimony was to the Jew alone (up to Acts 7) and thereafter throughout the rest of the book it was always to the Jew first. While the Church was there, its peculiar character was not made known until the Jew had finally rejected the renewed offer of the Kingdom, firstly from Peter in Jerusalem (see Acts 3: 19–21), then from Stephen (see Acts 7: 54–60) and finally from Paul in Rome, the capital of the Dispersion (see Acts 28: 23–31). The Jew was then set aside nationally "until the fulness of the nations be come in" (Rom. 11: 25).[30]

Now, while the Kingdom is in abeyance, in the sense of being established in power universally, the individual Jew not only comes into blessing ***on the same ground*** as the Gentile, but in the Church ***he has no priority.*** There, Gentile and Jew form "one new man" (Eph. 2: 15) as they are reconciled "in one body to God by the cross" (v16). That the nations would be blessed with the Jew under Christ in the

---

29 Incidentally, in the clause "but when that which is perfect has come", the Greek word for "that" (*to*) is in the neuter case which grammatically agrees with *musterion* (mystery) which is a neuter noun.

30 This fullness (*pleroma*) is the full complement from the Gentiles of the nations who now believe up to the point when God will lift the blindness of Israel. Then we will have the "fulness" of Israel (Rom. 11: 12) "when "all Israel shall be saved" (v26) and not just individuals as a remnant at the present time.

Kingdom was clearly taught in the OT prophets, but that Gentiles and Jews "should be joint heirs, and a joint body, and joint partakers of [his] promise in Christ Jesus by the glad tidings" (Eph. 3: 6) was previously unknown and forms one aspect of the Mystery. A Messiah present on earth in the midst of Israel was no secret but the subject of OT prophecy; a Christ rejected by Israel but glorified in heaven as "the head of the body, the assembly" (Col. 1: 18), united to that body on earth by the Holy Spirit, was unknown. This is a further aspect of the Mystery. No doubt Satan assumed that he was victorious when Christ was crucified and that his victory was reinforced when the Jew continued to reject the Man in the glory and the further offer of the Kingdom, ensuring the absence of Christ from the earth. However, God had purposed that the life of that blessed Man should be continued here, not personally, but characteristically in His body, the Church. This is the part of the Mystery referred to in the words "the riches of the glory of this mystery among the nations, which is Christ in you the hope of glory" (v27).

Even if Peter and John wrote after Paul, their subject matter was not unknown. The former wrote of the Kingdom, the latter of eternal life. Paul ***alone*** writes of the Mystery, the subject needed to complete the Word of God and to explain the present testimony consequent on the final rejection of the Kingdom by the Jew. Hence the Mystery is Gentile and Jew in one body on earth, forming one new man, united to Christ as Head in heaven by the Holy Spirit, continuing those blessed features that were seen in Christ personally as Man on earth. This truth could not be fully revealed until the Jew lost his priority in the testimony. Hence while the Mystery is mentioned in the appendix to Romans (see Rom. 16: 25-27—almost certainly written after the main epistle), we do not have the main details of it until the prison epistles of Ephesians and Colossians. Again, while it is true that we have the practical concept of the one body in the teachings of Romans and 1 Corinthians, there is no thought of the body united to the Head in heaven until we come to those prison epistles.

Now it is in relation to the Mystery that we have the thought of full knowledge and perfection. Paul desired that saints should be "united together in love, and unto all riches of the full assurance of understanding, to [the] full knowledge of the mystery of God" (Col. 2: 2). Earlier he had desired "that we may present every man perfect in Christ" (Col. 1: 28) and yet earlier still he had prayed "that ye may be filled with the full knowledge of his will, in all wisdom and spiritual understanding" (v9). Hence the gifts of the "word of wisdom" and the "word of knowledge" (1 Cor. 12: 8), so necessary when the full thought of the Mystery was unknown, are now redundant as what they rendered partially is now fully embraced in the Mystery "in which are hid ***all the treasures of wisdom and of knowledge***" (Col. 2: 3—my emphasis).

Further on we read that the new man is "renewed into full knowledge according to [the] image of him that has created him; wherein there is not Greek and Jew" (Col. 3: 10, 11). For the Ephesians, Paul desired that "the Father of glory, would give you [the] spirit of wisdom and revelation in the full knowledge of him" (Eph. 1: 17). The Mystery does not belong to the transitional state of the Church in its infancy where the Jew had priority nor to a carnal state like that at Corinth to which Paul said, "But we speak wisdom among the perfect" (1 Cor. 2: 6)—that is, the truth of the Mystery among those that are full–grown and mature). The Corinthians (like the Hebrews) were immature for Paul had to say, "I have given you milk to drink, not meat, for ye have not been able, nor indeed are ye yet able; for ye are yet carnal" (1 Cor. 3: 2, 3). Hence the teaching of 1 Cor. 13 is clear that certain temporary gifts would cease when the Mystery was made fully known.

**Summary**

I have sought to establish the following points from the Scriptures:

- It is only in the epistles written within the time span of the Acts that signs are spoken of
- Signs were given in connection with the establishment of the Kingdom in power on earth; the gifts belong to the Church
- "When that which is perfect has come" (1 Cor. 13: 10), the signs and a number of gifts would cease
- The phrase "that which is perfect" refers to the public introduction of the Mystery completing the body of truth in the Scriptures
- The Mystery is Gentile and Jew in one body on earth united by the Holy Spirit to Christ as Head in heaven

# Chapter 8

# The Present Time

## Introduction

The prophet Hosea had said "For the children of Israel shall abide many days without king, and without prince, and without sacrifice, and without statue, and without ephod and teraphim" (Hos. 3: 4) and this state began with the cessation of the sacrifices when both the temple and Jerusalem fell to Titus in AD70 under God's judgment. However, Paul asks "Has God cast away his people?" (Rom. 11: 1) and in his answer states that "in the present time also there has been a remnant according to election of grace" (v5) of whom Paul himself is a prime example (see v1) but "the rest have been blinded" (v7). The apostle does not wish us to be ignorant of this mystery "that blindness in part is happened to Israel, until the fulness of the nations be come in; and so all Israel shall be saved" (v25). This event awaits "The deliverer" ... who ... "shall turn away ungodliness from Jacob" (v26), that is, it awaits the return of Christ.

Now the signs[31], as we have seen, were for Israel. Hence if God, while saving individual Jews, is no longer dealing with Israel nationally then the signs have ceased. Accordingly, there is no mention of the word *signs* in any epistle written after the history of the Acts has closed but certain gifts are still referred to in Ephesians.

## The Gifts in Ephesians

Ephesians is the prison epistle in which, on the one hand, we have the Mystery spoken of in detail and, on the other hand, in which certain gifts are again brought before us. In chapter two Paul speaks of Gentile and Jew together in "one new man" (Eph. 2: 15) by the work of Christ who he says, "preached the glad tidings of peace to you who [were] afar off, and [the glad tidings of] peace to those [who were] nigh" (v17). The priority of the Jew has ended, and Paul shows this by

31 Exorcism, miracles, healings, tongues etc.

speaking of those afar off (Gentiles) before those that are nigh (Jews). Clearly in this epistle the apostle is speaking not of the local assembly but of the whole history of the Church from the giving of the gifts subsequent to the Lord's ascension (see Eph. 4: 8) "until we all arrive at the unity of the faith ... at [the] measure of the stature of the fulness of the Christ" (Eph. 4: 13). Only five gifts are listed, compared to seven in Romans (see Rom. 12: 4–8) and thirteen in Corinthians (see 1 Cor. 12: 8–10, 28–30). The only two gifts common to all three lists are those of prophecy and teaching. There are no continuing[32] signs in Ephesians for they belonged to the Kingdom and the Jew, not the Church and the Christian. The gifts are for the spiritual building up of the Church. But why do we have just these five gifts mentioned? The first two in the list are apostles and prophets and in relation to them Paul says that the Church is "being built upon the foundation of the apostles and prophets, Jesus Christ himself being the corner–stone" (Eph. 2: 20). Now beyond question, the start of any building is the foundation. When the foundations are laid and the building starts to rise, the foundations disappear from sight. Foundations are laid ***once*** and then are ***never seen again***. Such are the apostles and prophets. Their work is done. Not so with the corner–stone. Its purpose is to ensure that the building is "four–square" (see Rev. 21: 16) and it is there for the builders to take their bearing from. Thus Christ, the corner–stone, is ever there but the apostles and prophets are no more (no matter what some may claim).

Once the foundation was laid, what of the rise of the building, what of its continuance? The work begun by the apostles and prophets was continued by evangelists, shepherds, and teachers. The evangelist secures the material for the building by the salvation of souls. Once in the Church, those saved need to be taught "the faith once delivered to the saints" (Jude v3) and preserved in the Scriptures and cared for in the light of that teaching by the shepherds. Thus, the only major[33]

---

[32] Prophets and apostles are foundational (see Eph. 2: 20), but evangelists, shepherds and teachers are gifts and are never spoken of as signs.

[33] From 1 Cor. 12: 31, it is clear that the gifts were graded. Prophecy was a major gift, its essential feature being one called by God to speak for God. In both the OT and the NT it involved the revelation of future events (see Acts 11: 27, 28) and also exhortation (see Acts 15: 32). Now exhortation itself was a gift in its own right, distinct from prophecy (compare Rom. 12: 6 with Rom. 12: 8). Hence prophecy, a major gift, embraced exhortation, a minor gift. While prophecy, in the full sense of the gift involving the revelation of future events, is no more, we still have the gift of exhortation. Likewise, the listing of the major gifts of the evangelist, the shepherd and the

gifts remaining today are evangelists, pastors and teachers. In keeping with this when Peter issues his warning to Jewish Christians, he says "But there were false prophets also among the people", (referring to Israel in the OT) "as there shall be also among you false teachers" (2 Pet. 2: 1). He does not say "false prophets" in the second clause but "false teachers" for, as Peter writes after the history of Acts had closed, his readers would know that the gift of the prophet had been withdrawn from the Church.

**The Great Deception**

At the present time Israel is set aside in judgment (see Rom. 11: 15), but after the Church is raptured to heaven (see 1 Thess. 4: 13–18), God will recommence his dealings with Israel. Commensurate with those dealings will be the revelation of the Antichrist. This is detailed in the last book of the Bible in figurative language. Accordingly, with the reappearance of Israel nationally, we have signs once more and Israel again takes priority over the Gentile (compare vs. 4 and 9 in Rev. 7).

Now the very title Antichrist tells us that this man will be the embodiment of everything that is against (anti) the true Christ. To accomplish this, the deception must be almost perfect. As the real Christ came to the Jew, so the Antichrist will come to the same people and establish his credentials by performing the OT signs predicted of the real Christ. However, before ***the*** Antichrist appears there will be many false Christs and false prophets as the Lord Himself warned: "For there shall arise false Christs, and false prophets, and shall give great signs and wonders, so as to mislead, if possible, even the elect" (Matt. 24: 24). Now there is absolutely nothing to suggest that such signs and wonders will not be genuine displays of supernatural power. Indeed, there is great danger of the elect (that is real believers among the Jews) being deceived. Even in the Apostle John's day, John warned ***Christian*** believers that "it is [the] last hour, and, according as ye have heard that antichrist comes, even now there have come many antichrists" (1 John 2: 18). In 2 Thess. 2: 3–12, Paul tells us more about the Antichrist, the man of sin, the son of perdition, saying "that he himself sits down in the temple of God" (2 Thess. 2: 4), showing that

---

teacher does not mean that service, giving, leading, showing mercy, helps, governments and faith are no more.

as the Jewish temple was still standing when Paul wrote, it will again be there (see Rev. 11: 1) when the Antichrist appears. The coming of the Antichrist will be "according to the working of Satan in all power and signs and wonders of falsehood" (2 Thess. 2: 9). Note well the three Satanic marks of deception that will be employed: "power" (*dunamesin*), "signs" (*semeios*) and "wonders" (*terasin*). ***These are the same three things, using exactly the same Greek words, that God employed to bear witness to those that confirmed the word of the Lord in Heb. 2: 4***: "both by signs and wonders, and various acts of power". Hence the counterfeit will be near perfect. Also note the word "all" in 2 Thess. 2: 9. Will there be miracles? Yes! Will there be healings? Certainly! Will there be the ***apparent*** casting out of demons? Yes, because if this were not so the deception would not be complete, for that word *all* in this context has the meaning of *every kind of*. Surely though in the light of Matt. 12: 26, there cannot be the actual casting out of demons? While the words "of falsehood" in 2 Thess. 2: 9 may indicate that not all the signs are genuine, it does not in anyway alter the fact that the signs will be ***accepted*** as genuine and that men will be ***deceived***—which is the Antichrist's grand object. ***The testimony is false***, whether or not all the signs are genuine.

Now notice two further points in 2 Thess. 2. The Antichrist is referred to as "the lawless one" (v8) and we are told that "the mystery of lawlessness already works" (v7) and this was in the time of the Acts![34] This brings us to a most solemn Scripture: Matt. 7: 21–23.

### The Miracle Workers of Matthew Seven

As this Scripture is so important and has a direct bearing on our subject, I shall quote it in full:

> Not every one who says to me, Lord, Lord, shall enter into the kingdom of the heavens, but he that does the will of my Father who is in the heavens. Many shall say to me in that day, Lord, Lord, have we not prophesied through *thy* name, and through *thy* name cast out demons, and through *thy* name done many works of

[34] For the Thessalonian epistles were written when the temple was still standing (see 2 Thess. 2: 4).

> power? And then will I avow unto them, I never knew you. Depart from me, workers of lawlessness. (Matt. 7: 21–23).

The full force of the Lord's awful condemnation is enhanced by realising what He does not say. He does not refute the claim of these workers of lawlessness to have prophesied in His name, He does not deny that they had cast out demons in His name, and He does not dispute that they had done many works of power in His name. ***None of their claims are challenged, let alone refuted***. Again, He does not deny that they had used His name. Furthermore, He does not call them liars or hypocrites. He calls them "workers of lawlessness". Why? Because they had the main characteristic of the Antichrist—***the*** lawless one (see 2 Thess. 2: 8)—they did their own will and not the Father's will. I say again, there is absolutely nothing in the passage to throw any doubt on their claims. They really did what they said they did—***but it was not according to God's will***. Contrast this with the testimony of "those who have heard; God bearing, besides, witness with [them] to [it], both by signs and wonders, and various acts of power, and distributions of [the] Holy Spirit, ***according to his will***" (Heb. 2: 4—my emphasis). That is the key to the whole matter, and I will enlarge on this in a moment. However, before I do so I must address the difficulty that some may have in accepting that unbelievers, such as those in Matt. 7, can perform miracles in the name of the Lord. The response could be compressed to a single word: Judas! This man is a specific example of an unbeliever exercising divine power by working miracles and performing signs. It says of the twelve (and hence Judas is included) that the Lord "gave them power over unclean spirits, so that they should cast them out, and heal every disease and every bodily weakness" (Matt. 10: 1). The twelve went out in pairs (see Mark 6: 7) so that somebody went with Judas, leaving us in no doubt that all twelve "cast out many demons, and anointed with oil many infirm, and healed them" (v13). Thus, having miraculous powers given by God in no way accredits the recipient as a believer.

## The Will of God

Earlier in the booklet, when I asked why the Lord Jesus came, I suggested that many would respond with 1 Tim. 1: 15—that He came to save sinners. While this is perfectly true, I pointed out that He also came to confirm the promises to the fathers according to Rom. 15: 8, 9. However, there is something that takes precedence over both of these reasons for his coming and, indeed, over everything else, for He said "Lo, I come (in [the] roll of the book it is written of me) to do, O God, thy will" (Heb. 10: 7) and again, "For I am come down from heaven, not that I should do *my* will, but the will of him that has sent me" (John 6: 38). In a word, the Lord came to do the will of God. Every word He spoke, everything he did, had to be subject to this question: Was it in the will of God? Every miracle performed and every sickness cured was only carried out because it was the will of God to do so—because it was God's time for the signs for Israel. When the Lord sent out the twelve and later the seventy, to perform miracles, He did so because it was in God's will. When Judas healed the sick, he was carrying out the will of God—even though he did not believe. After the Lord ascended and the apostles went forth and again performed the same miracles, they carried out the will of God in doing so, as Heb. 2: 4 explicitly states—for again, it was one of the times of the signs. However, when those spoken of in Matt. 7 performed miracles, the Lord describes them as workers of lawlessness because they did not do "the will of my Father who is in the heavens" (v21). It was then not one of the times of the signs. ***Matt. 7 proves that men may do miracles in the Lord's name but not do the will of God in doing so***. I ask, if unbelievers can perform miracles without doing the will of God, cannot genuine believers do the same? Where does that place the so–called 'end–time apostles and prophets' of today? Where does that leave the 'faith–healers' and 'tongue–speakers' of the present time? I leave my reader to supply the answer.

Now while this word of the Lord in Matt. 7 may have its prime bearing on the Jew of a future day, Paul writes to Christians of one who does "his own will in humility and worship of angels" (Col. 2: 18), stating elsewhere that such need to "awake up out of the snare of the devil, [who are] taken by him, for *his* will" (2 Tim. 2: 26). The believer is to "be not foolish, but understanding what [is] the will of the Lord" (Eph. 5: 17) for God has "made known to us the mystery of his will" (Eph. 1: 9). We are exhorted to:

> ... be filled with the full knowledge of his will, in all wisdom and spiritual understanding, [so as] to walk worthily of the Lord unto all well–pleasing, bearing

> fruit in every good work, and growing by the true knowledge of God.
> (Col. 1: 9, 10).

***The will of God does not involve the exercise of signs now for today is not one of the times of the signs***.

**A Final Word from Deuteronomy**

God may be using the claims of the Pentecostal/Charismatic movement to test the affections of Christians in the same way as He did His earthly people. Bearing in mind that the "things as have been written before have been written for our instruction" (Rom. 15: 4), let us turn to Deut. 13:

> If there arise among you a prophet, or one that dreameth dreams, and he give thee a sign or a wonder, and the sign or the wonder come to pass that he told unto thee, when he said, Let us go after other gods, whom thou hast not known, and let us serve them,—thou shalt not hearken unto the words of that prophet, or that dreamer of dreams; ***for Jehovah your God proveth you, to know whether ye love Jehovah your God with all your heart and with all your soul***.
> (Deut. 13: 1–3—my emphasis).

As this false prophet arose from among the people, he was an Israelite. However, he was also apostate for his object was to get Israel to serve other gods—idols. Could such a thing happen in Christianity? One of the last of the NT epistles closes with the warning "Children, keep yourselves from idols" (1 John 5: 21) and an idol for the Christian is anything that takes the eye off Christ. Now to give credence to his words, this prophet or dreamer spoken of in Deut. 13 gave a sign or a wonder, and the sign or wonder actually came to pass. Yet he "hath spoken revolt against Jehovah your God" (Deut. 13: 5) for his object was to "draw thee out of the way that Jehovah thy God commanded thee to walk in" (v5). In other words, he would take them away from the will of God. Israel had had a clear word from Jehovah "Hear, Israel: Jehovah our God is one Jehovah; and thou shalt love Jehovah thy God with all thy heart, and with all thy soul, and with all thy strength"

(Deut. 6: 4, 5). They had God's Word. This man backed up what he said with a sign or wonder. Should they believe God or man? That was the issue. It is the selfsame issue today. Are we to be swayed by signs, miracles, and wonders, or are we to rest on the Word of God? Such a dreamer or prophet was to be "put to death; for he hath spoken revolt against Jehovah your God" (Deut. 13: 5). Yet the sign was genuine. There is nothing in the passage to suggest that the sign was false. The word was false, but the sign real. Why would this occur? Why may there be signs and the like today? "For Jehovah your God proveth you, to know whether ye love Jehovah your God with all your heart and with all your soul" (v3). ***The conclusion that one must draw is that the claims of men to own Christ as Lord and to substantiate those claims by miracles is no guarantee whatsoever that those claims are genuine. Signs are not the will of God at the present time***.

**Summary**

I have sought to establish the following points from the Scriptures:

- God is not dealing with Israel nationally and hence there are no signs from God at the present time
- The gifts in Ephesians are given in relation to the universal building up of the Church
- Of the five gifts listed in Ephesians, the apostles and prophets are clearly stated to be the foundation and hence exist no more
- The only three ***major*** gifts in existence today are the evangelist, the shepherd and the teacher
- When the Antichrist appears, he will perform the same signs that the Lord Jesus performed
- There are antichrists today who, while they may perform miracles, do not do the will of God
- The will of God is the supreme test, as illustrated by Matt. 7: 21–23
- The performance of signs is not the will of God at the present time
- God may be testing the affections of His people today, as He did Israel of old, to see whether they would rather believe miracles or His Word

# Chapter 9

# Summing Up

**Overall Summary**

The major points in the booklet that I have sought to establish from the Scriptures are as follows:

- The signs are identified with Israel and the Jew
- The Lord Jesus came initially as the Messiah (the Christ) to the Jew to establish the Kingdom in power on earth
- The signs were miracles prophesied in the OT to accredit Jesus as the Christ and showed the imminence of the Kingdom
- Subsequent to the Lord's ascension, the testimony of the Kingdom and of Jesus as the Christ continued with the apostles
- The apostles' testimony was accompanied by the same signs that were given before the Lord's crucifixion with the addition of the sign of tongues
- The additional sign of tongues was given to warn the Jew of coming national judgment
- While the testimony was restricted to Jerusalem and the Jew, the signs were given in abundance by the apostles
- When the testimony went out to the Samaritans and the Gentiles, the Jew still had priority and the signs continued but were less frequent
- While the Church was present from Acts 2 onwards, the testimony was still of the Kingdom and there was no public testimony of the Mystery
- Throughout Acts, while the Jew had priority, the Church was still publicly linked with Judaism
- While the signs are identified with the Jew and the Kingdom, the gifts are identified with the Christian and the Church

- Certain signs were also gifts and certain gifts were connected with the foundation of the Church
- The words "when that which is perfect has come" (1 Cor. 13: 10) refer to the completeness of the Word of God supplied by the truth of the Mystery
- When the Jew was set aside in judgment and the truth of the Mystery was made known publicly, the signs ceased along with the gifts connected with the foundation of the Church
- It is not the will of God for signs at the present time
- Miracles done in the Lord's name can be performed by those who do not know Him
- When God begins His dealings again with the Jew, the signs will recommence, along with false signs and the revelation of the Antichrist
- Hence miracles do not prove that the power exercised is of God

**Conclusions**

It has well been said that Satan has only two lines of attack on the testimony of God: he either opposes it outright, resulting in persecution for those who give it, or he seeks to corrupt it. In Acts 13 Satan used Elymas the magician, a false prophet, to oppose the testimony of Paul in the Gospel, but in Acts 16 Satan changed his tactics and used a certain female slave with a spirit of Python to testify that these men "are bondmen of the Most High God, who announce to you [the] way of salvation" (Acts 16: 17). The latter course is far more difficult to deal with. It is what faces us in regard to current claims to speak with tongues, to heal the sick and to perform signs and miracles. I do not doubt that there are genuine believers who are not only caught up in this movement but who are also actively engaged in promulgating it. Some of its leaders are being used of God for the spiritual blessing of men in the Gospel. That does not make the miracles genuine or establish God as their source. The Scriptures are the only yardstick.

As mentioned earlier, we never read of signs in any epistle written after the history of the Acts has closed. In those epistles we read, not of miracles of healing, but of saints being sick. If Paul could still exercise the gift of healing (as he did previously), how strange it is to hear him tell Timothy to "use a little wine on account of thy stomach and thy frequent illnesses" (1 Tim. 5: 23). Another saint, Epaphroditus, "was also sick close to death, but God had mercy on him" (Phil. 2: 27). This healing was not the result of the exercise of any gift, but of God showing mercy. Then Paul says "Trophimus I left behind in Miletus sick" (2 Tim. 4: 20). This was not within the time of the Acts, for then (see Acts 20: 15–17) he was well and accompanied Paul to Jerusalem (see Acts 21: 29). Trophimus was left behind at Miletus after Paul's first release from prison and subsequent missionary journey, of which Scripture gives just scant details. Why did Paul leave him behind? The only answer is that the gift of healing was no longer being exercised. Again, if healings abounded, as in the beginning of Acts, why does Paul speak of "Luke, the beloved physician" (Col. 4: 14)? Why does a man need to be described in relation to his medical skills if the Church has the gift of healing? It is not that God does not heal sicknesses but that the Church no longer has the gift of healing. It is not that the Lord may not give a word of a prophetic character[35] in the local assembly but that prophets, in the full meaning of the word, are no longer needed because, with the revelation of the Mystery, the Scriptures are complete. It is not that the Lord may not send some servant on a particular mission but that the apostles (again in the full meaning of the word) are no more. Judaism had one apostle (Moses—see Heb. 3: 1–3) who established that system and after he died it had no further apostles. Likewise, the apostles of Christianity are its foundation and now are no more. As to tongues, they have ceased as they are no longer needed, for God's judgment has fallen on Israel and they are still set aside in the ways of God.

Yet my reader may persist and say that the claims to the phenomena of prophecy and healing surely show that these gifts still exist in the Church. As I said at the beginning, I do not need to verify whether or not these take place, I only need to check from the Scriptures whether it is in the mind of God for these signs and gifts to continue. I have sought to demonstrate that the Scriptures clearly show that they exist no longer. However, before we parallel today's phenomena alongside what we have in the Scriptures to see if they correspond, let us parallel the gift of evangelism with what we have in the Bible—for few would deny the continuance of the gift of the evangelist.

---

[35] That is, God may use a servant to bring the Word of God, the Scriptures, to bear on the particular circumstances of certain of His people.

The evangelist in the Scriptures gave outstanding service in the sphere of the Gospel as "Philip the evangelist" (Acts 21: 8) did both to the crowds and the individual (see Acts 8), and as Peter did when thousands were saved (see Acts 2: 41; 4: 4). Have we not men today who do the same? Thank God that we have—the gift of the evangelist is still with us. The parallel is there. But what of the gifts of prophecy and healing? Let us take prophecy first. Prophecies abound in the Pentecostal/Charismatic movement and the so–called prophets are legion. One prominent among them claims that "if I hit two–thirds [of prophecies coming true], I'm doing pretty good". How does a two–thirds success rate compare with the prophets of the Bible?

> But the prophet who shall presume to speak a word in my name that I have not commanded him to speak, or that shall speak in the name of other gods, that prophet shall die ... When a prophet speaketh in the name of Jehovah, and the thing followeth not, nor cometh to pass, that is the word which Jehovah hath not spoken; the prophet hath spoken it presumptuously: be not afraid of him.
> (Deut. 18: 20, 22).

Bible prophecies were one hundred per cent correct.[36] Prophecies that are less than that do not come from God. Such was the seriousness of the matter that the penalty for speaking presumptuously in the OT was death. There are no prophets today. Hence there can be no longer any speaking "in revelation, or in knowledge, or in prophecy" (1 Cor. 14: 6) but only "in teaching" (v6) of that which has already been made known.

Let us now consider the gift of healing. Peter clearly had the gift of healing. Indeed, such was the distinctiveness of his gift "that they brought out the sick into the streets and put [them] on beds and couches, that at least the shadow of Peter, when he came, might

[36] A well–known Pentecostal has sought to defend the position that all prophecies need not be one hundred per cent correct by claiming that the prophecy of Agabus (see Acts 21: 11) was not accurately fulfilled for the Romans actually bound Paul and not the Jews as prophesied (see Acts 21: 33). Well then, let us run a parallel. Clearly, the Romans and not the Jews physically crucified Christ. Yet Peter says to the Jews "Jesus Christ the Nazaraean, whom ye have crucified" (Acts 4: 10). Was Peter mistaken? No! The Jews were responsible for the death of Christ just as they also were responsible for putting Paul in chains. Hence the prophecy of Agabus was one hundred per cent accurate.

overshadow some one of them" (Acts 5: 15). Does this happen with any of today's healers? No, for they haven't got the gift. The Scripture just quoted goes on to say, "who were all healed" (v16). Peter had no healing failures. ***In fact, the NT does not record a single failure in the exercise of the gift of healing***. Is that the situation with the Pentecostal/Charismatic movement? The history of this movement is littered with failures. There is just no parallel with today's claims of men exercising the gift of healing and what took place as recorded in the Bible. As with Peter, so with Paul, of whom it was said "so that even napkins or aprons were brought from his body [and put] upon the sick, and the diseases left them" (Acts 19: 12). Please note that the argument is not that healings do not take place today, but that the gift of healing is no more. God is sovereign and has ever intervened miraculously when it was His will to do so (for example, Hezekiah secured another 15 years of life as a result of his prayer—see 2 Kings 20: 1–11) but this was the exception, not the rule). Those who think that they have the gift of healing are sadly deluded, and even sadder is the fact that they delude others.

Finally, the fact that such miracles may take place does not mean that they come from God or that they take place as a result of His will. The words of the Lord in Matt. 7 identifying those who will enter the Kingdom are "he that does the will of my Father who is in the heavens" (Matt. 7: 21). The question that needs to be asked is 'Is it in the divine will that such miracles should take place at the present time and mark the day?' We have seen from the Scriptures that the answer is ***NO***. That God may in His sovereignty work miracles of healing for individuals, I do not doubt. ***But the present time is not one of the times of the signs, it is not the age of miracles***. As to those who claim to work miracles of one kind or another, we must leave them to God.

Again, while the present time is ***NOT*** one of the times of the signs, this does not mean that God does not do miracles. Every conversion to Christ is supernatural and thus a miracle. These spiritual miracles last—for all eternity; physical miracles (such as healing) do not go beyond death. ***Sadly, men (and, even sadder, some saints of God) would rather have physical miracles than spiritual ones***!

# Appendices

## 1: The Meaning of the Word *Tongues* in Scripture

The Greek word used for tongues either means the organ of speech resident in the mouth of a person or a spoken language. Now while the Pentecostal/Charismatic movement is forced by the wording of Acts 2 to admit that the tongues spoken there were real languages, many among them would claim that the tongues spoken of as a gift in the first Corinthian epistle were not human languages at all but exuberant, ecstatic spiritual utterances (utterances, incidentally, that they must share with other modern religions like the Mormons, as well as the pagan temple mediums at the oracle of Delphi not far from Corinth in Paul's day!). This argument is also used by some outside of the Pentecostal/Charismatic movement. They point out that such phenomena often took place at the great evangelical revivals in the past. As these revivals are rightly accepted as the work of God, they feel the need to justify the accompanying phenomena from the Bible. They forget that when God works, Satan is not idle either.

Now the supposed Scriptural grounds for this change from the real languages of Acts 2 to unintelligible utterances is said to be determined by whether the word for tongues is singular or plural, and whether it is coupled with a singular or plural subject. Thus, for example, in 1 Cor. 14 where we have the words "he that speaks with a tongue" (v2), because the word "tongue" is in the singular with a singular subject "he", we are to understand an ecstatic utterance. Likewise, where we have the plural word "tongues" with a plural subject, such as "all" in "all speak with tongues" (v23), we again are to understand ecstatic utterances. However, in the same chapter where we have the words "if I come to you speaking with tongues" (v6) because the word "tongues" is now in the plural but with a singular subject "I", normal languages are meant. This interpretation, according to one advocate, makes 1 Cor. 14: 2, 4, 5, 13, 14, 19, 23, 26,

27 to be ecstatic utterances but 1 Cor. 14: 6, 18[37], 21, 22 normal ethnic languages. There is one Greek word in v22 that demolishes this theological theory—*oste*. This word is used to summarise and draw conclusions from a previous argument and in English is expressed by the words *so that*. If the previous argument had been between two different kinds of tongues (real languages and ecstatic utterances), then v22 introduced by *oste* (*so that*) would have been a comparison between these two kinds of tongues. It is not. The verse reads "So that tongues are for a sign, not to those who believe, but to unbelievers; but prophecy, not to unbelievers, but to those who believe" (v22). The comparison in the apostle's summary is between tongues and prophecy, for Paul was previously comparing and contrasting tongues and prophecy, not two different kinds of tongues.

Lastly, if the tongues exercised by the Corinthians were the same as those practised by the priestesses a few miles away in Delphi's pagan temple, why did the Corinthians make so much of them—for, at best, it only made them the peers of idolaters? As mentioned already, ecstatic ungrammatical outbursts are common to many religions, ancient and modern, of which God is most certainly not the Author.

---

[37] However, in the better Greek manuscripts v18 is in the singular sending this verse to the ecstatic side of the so–called divide!

# 2: The Meaning of "when that which is perfect has come" (1 Cor. 13: 10)

The common interpretation of the words "when that which is perfect has come" (1 Cor. 13: 10) is that they refer to the moment when the Church will be complete at the return of the Lord Jesus. This interpretation states that all the gifts will remain here "until we all arrive at the unity of the faith and of the knowledge of the Son of God, at [the] full–grown man, at [the] measure of the stature of the fulness of the Christ" (Eph. 4: 13).

Now it must be acknowledged that both 1 Cor. 13 and Eph. 4 have similar terms: *gifts*, *perfection*, *knowledge* and *babes* (plural of *nepios*—which is the same Greek word as *child*. ***However, similarity in terms does not prove identity in meaning***. Certainly, the whole history of the Church is before us in Eph. 4, from the ascension of Christ and the giving of the gifts (see vs. 8–11) "until we all arrive ..." (v13). If Eph. 4 is a true parallel to 1 Cor. 13, then "that which is perfect" in 1 Cor. 13: 10 must equate to "[the] full–grown man" of Eph. 4: 13. Certainly the Greek word *teleion* can be translated *perfect* (as in 1 Cor. 13: 10), *complete* or *full–grown* (as in Eph. 4: 13), depending on the context. Thus, so far there is a parallel. Again, when Paul says, "but then shall I know according as I also have been known" (1 Cor. 13: 12) the knowledge he is referring to is complete for it is contrasted with "now I know partially" (v12). The Greek word for *know* in the former clause is *epiginosko* which means *full knowledge* and not just *knowledge* (*ginosko*) as in the latter clause of v12. The word used in Eph. 4: 13 for the "knowledge" of the Son of God is the noun from *epiginosko*. Again, we have a sound parallel. But then in 1 Cor. 13 we find that Paul uses an example to illustrate the previous verse where he says, "but when that which is perfect has come, then that which is in part shall be done away" (v10). Hence if the interpretation is correct then the state illustrated by "a child" in "When I was a child ... when I became a man" (v11) must belong to the ***present time*** and the state illustrated by "a man" must be relegated to ***the future*** when the Church is complete. However, returning to Eph. 4, I find that not only are the gifts in that chapter there "until we all arrive at the unity of the faith and of the knowledge of the Son of God" (when the Church is complete), "at [the] full–grown man, at [the] measure of the stature of the fulness of the Christ" (v13), but Paul goes on to say that these gifts are "in order that we may be no longer babes ... but, holding the truth in love, we may grow up to him in all things" (vs. 14–15). Now, as already mentioned, that word *babes* is identical to the word for *child* in the singular in 1 Cor. 13: 11. While ***collectively*** all will not reach full growth or manhood until the Church is complete, ***individually*** at the present time we are most definitely not meant to remain babes. It was said to the Hebrews,

> For when for the time ye ought to be teachers, ye have again need that [one] should teach you what [are] the elements of the beginning of the oracles of God, and have become such as have need of milk, [and] not of solid food. For every one that partakes of milk [is] unskilled in the word of righteousness, for he is a babe; but solid food belongs to full–grown men. (Heb. 5: 12–14).

As they were babes, they are exhorted to "go on [to what belongs] to full growth" (Heb. 6: 1). Thus, the supposed parallel is false. Again, if knowledge cannot be complete now, the apostle's prayer "that ye may be filled with the ***full*** knowledge of his will, in all wisdom and spiritual understanding" (Col. 1: 9—my emphasis) cannot be answered at the present time. Nor can believers be "renewed into ***full*** knowledge" (Col. 3: 10—my emphasis) or have "the ***full*** assurance of understanding, to [the] ***full*** knowledge of the mystery of God" (Col. 2: 2—my emphasis).

Yet again, the supposed parallel of 1 Cor. 13 with Eph. 4 is only superficial because in the latter Scripture the gifts are there "until we all arrive at the unity of the faith"—the movement, the arriving, is ours—we arrive; whereas in the former Scripture it is "when that which is perfect" ***has come***—that is the movement is of "that which is perfect", not ours.

Finally, while there is a time limit in both 1 Cor. 13 and Eph. 4, the bias of the presentation in the former is linked with what is done away while in the latter it is towards what continues ("until"—Eph. 4: 13). Thus, the apparent parallel between the two Scriptures is not correct and the interpretation of the words "when that which is perfect has come" (1 Cor. 13: 10) as referring to the completion of the Church is wrong.

# 3: The Purpose of Tongues

It is a sad fact that what we believe as Christians may be influenced not only by Scripture, but by tradition, experience, speculation and even prejudice. Our attitude to the subject of 'tongues' is a pertinent example. To arrive at the truth, we must clear away this raft of human ideas and thoughts and concentrate ***solely*** on what God has said in His Word. Our attitude to the evidence revealed therein will demonstrate, like nothing else can, the spiritual state of our souls.

Contrary to popular belief, there is no actual evidence that the gift of tongues (or languages) was given to ***aid*** the spread of the Gospel message. This may have been a useful ***effect*** of tongues, but effect is not purpose. Indeed, we read of only three historical occasions on which the gift was used (see Acts 2: 4–13; 10: 44–46; 19: 6)—somewhat surprising in view of the detailed accounts of the many places evangelised given to us by Luke. (The idea that there are many unrecorded instances is pure speculation, as is the theory that what Simon the magician ***saw*** in Acts 8: 18 involved tongues). Furthermore, in Acts 10 Peter ***preached*** and in Acts 19 Paul ***conversed*** but neither spoke in tongues. It was their converted listeners that spoke in tongues. Furthermore, in Acts 10 all those spoken to in tongues were already converted (10: 23, 45; 11: 12), and had also just listened without difficulty to Peter preaching in his ***native*** tongue. Tongues can hardly be said to be an evangelistic tool there!

The first mention of tongues in the NT is a prophetic one—Mark 16: 17–20—and indicates their special character. Tongues were not only an expression of divine power but were for a sign: "And these signs shall follow those that have believed: in my name they shall cast out demons; they shall speak with new tongues ..." (v17). They had a message to convey. In this context they were a witness to the authenticity of the preaching. This is corroborated by verse 20: "confirming the word by the signs following upon [it]". Why did the word need to be confirmed? Because it was ***new***, that is, the signs were to be a witness to the fact that this new 'religion' that had arisen was of God. Of course this would be particularly applicable to the Jew who would need to have any departure from the divinely accredited faith he was practising confirmed.

This idea of tongues being for a sign is expanded by the Apostle Paul: "It is written in the law, By people of other tongues, and by strange lips, will I speak to this people; and neither thus will they hear me, saith the Lord. So that tongues are for a sign, not to those who believe, but to unbelievers" (1 Cor. 14: 21, 22). The OT Scripture to which Paul refers is Is. 28: 11, 12: "For with stammering lips and a strange tongue will he speak to this people". The persons there addressed are the unbelieving Israelites of Isaiah's day ("this people"), and the message conveyed is one of ***impending judgement***. Thus, the passage continues: "that they might go, and fall backward, and be broken, and snared, and taken" (v13). The strange tongue referred to is that of the soon–coming army of Babylon.[38] Much the same message is conveyed by Jer. 5: 15 and Deut. 28: 49. Indeed if we go back to the origin of tongues, we find that they were first introduced in the judgement of God (see Gen. 11: 1–9). Tongues then, appear to be peculiarly connected with judgement.

Now the picture presented by Isaiah is not one in which the communications between the Babylonians and the Israelites were of the highest quality. We read of a "strange tongue"—an unfamiliar language, namely Chaldean—and "stammering lips"—persons struggling to speak in a foreign language (in this case, Babylonians trying to speak Hebrew). Why should Paul quote such a passage if he meant to convey that the purpose of the gift of tongues was to ***aid*** the spread of the Christian message? Those who heard the Gospel on the day of Pentecost did not hear "strange tongues" or "stammering lips". On the contrary, they heard familiar tongues—their own native languages. Indeed, more than that, they heard each in "his own dialect" (Acts 2: 6), implying competence in the language. No, the reason the apostle quotes Is. 28 is to show that tongues are a ***sign***.

At whom was this sign primarily aimed? In Isaiah's day, to hear a strange language was a sign of impending judgement. It was a sign to those who did not understand, or at least had difficulty in understanding, the tongue. On the day of Pentecost, while tongue–speaking had a great effect on those who understood it (see Acts 2: 12), as a sign it was aimed at those who did not. For them, as in Isaiah's day, it was a sign of judgement.

---

[38] Isaiah 28 relates both to Assyria (in respect of Ephraim) and Babylon (in respect of Judah). The seventh and fourteenth verses are connected.

The company of Jews which heard the disciples speak can be divided into two, namely ***native–born*** and ***foreign–born***. The foreign–born Jews were a product of the dispersion, and though many would know Hebrew, their first language would have been that of the country in which they had been born. To have heard Peter and his fellow–apostles speaking in Hebrew would have been natural enough, but to hear them speak in their own tongues filled them with amazement.

Also present in the crowd listening to the disciples, however, were "others" who "mocking said, They are full of new wine" (v13). From Peter's response it is evident that these others were local or native–born Jews: "Men of Judaea, and all ye inhabitants of Jerusalem, let this be known to you, and give heed to my words: for these are not full of wine, as ye suppose" (vs 14, 15). Now since the apostles were speaking in foreign languages, these Jews, knowing only Hebrew (or Aramaic) would only hear unintelligible speech. Foolishly, they dismissed this expression of the gift of God as the ramblings of drunkards when they ought to have seen it as a sign that judgement was coming upon Israel. As unbelievers and as those who did not understand the tongues, the sign was particularly for them. Why was judgement coming? Because a perverse generation of Jews had crucified and slain their own Messiah (significantly, Peter quotes from a passage in Joel that has in view the "day of [the] Lord" (Acts 2: 20)—a day of judgement). It is to these native–born Jews that Peter drives his message home: "him, given up by the determinate counsel and foreknowledge of God, ye, by [the] hand of lawless [men], have crucified and slain ... this Jesus whom ye have crucified" (vs. 23, 36).

The second recorded occurrence of the gift of tongues is on the introduction of the testimony to the Gentiles. Unlike at Pentecost, in Acts 10 there are ***no*** unbelieving Jews present (or indeed any unbelievers at all) when the tongue–speaking takes place. However, it was still a sign. The "faithful of the circumcision were astonished" (v45) that God had acknowledged ***uncircumcised*** men as His people. They could not question this because the evidence was plain to see: "for they heard them speaking with tongues and magnifying God" (v46). Was not circumcision necessary to enter the sphere of blessing? Did not one have to be an Israelite in order to be accounted as part of the people of God? That the uncircumcised had spoken in tongues could only mean that God was setting the nation aside—and if it was being set aside it could only be for judgement. Did the faithful of the circumcision believe this, or did they cling to the idea of Christianity being just an updated version of Judaism? Judgement was now the only future for Judaism. What spoke of blessing for the Gentiles, spoke of judgement for the nation. Blessing for individual Jews was still available but blessing for the nation had gone.

On returning to Jerusalem, Peter is met by unbelief: "Thou wentest in to men uncircumcised and hast eaten with them" (Acts 11: 3). Peter answers these Jewish opposers by asserting that "the Holy Spirit fell upon them even as upon us also at the beginning" (v15)—that is, accompanied by the speaking in tongues (compare Acts 2: 4). Previously salvation had been "of the Jews" (John 4: 22), now it was to be extended (see Acts 11: 14), and the fact that uncircumcised Gentiles were given the Holy Spirit was a witness to Judaism that their system was no longer where salvation was to be found. Peter uses the sign of Gentiles speaking in tongues to witness to the nation that circumcision was now irrelevant.

The last historical mention of tongues is in Acts 19—the introduction of the twelve disciples of John at Ephesus into the Assembly. That there were many Jews in the vicinity is seen by the fact that immediately afterwards Paul entered into the synagogue (see v8). For John's disciples to speak in tongues accredited both John's message, and the link between it and Christianity. John's message was ***exclusively*** Jewish, but though that word was authentic, it was now superseded by a more inclusive message. Some Jews "were hardened and disbelieved" (v9) however, and so Paul "left them and separated the disciples, reasoning daily in the school of Tyrannus" (v9).

Tongue–speaking also took place in the Assembly in Corinth, but Paul neither commends nor condemns it. What he does take issue with is the absence of translation (see 1 Cor. 14: 5–13, 28). Now it can hardly be imagined that to speak in tongues was merely the random utterance of unrelated words in a foreign language—a sensible, intelligent speaking is implied (compare verses 16 and 17). If this foreign language was not translated, what was the profit to the Assembly, or, as Paul puts it, "how shall he who fills the place of the simple [Christian] say Amen, at thy giving of thanks, since he does not know what thou sayest?" (v16). The apostle had great ability in tongues but when he took his place in the Assembly he deliberately refrained from speaking in that way. He would rather speak in that which was intelligible to others: "I thank God I speak in a tongue more than all of you: but in [the] assembly I desire to speak five words with my understanding, that I may instruct others also, [rather] than ten thousand words in a tongue" (vs. 18, 19). It is wrong to say that Paul did not value tongues, but he knew that their real place lay ***outside*** the Assembly: "So that tongues are for a sign, not to those who believe, but to unbelievers" (v22). Now unbelievers did on occasion come into the Assembly as verse 23 shows, and so Paul did not forbid the speaking with tongues (see v39), but he clearly felt that the more appropriate gift to be expressed in the Assembly was prophecy: "Now I desire that ye should all speak with tongues, but rather that ye should prophesy. But greater is he that prophesies than he that speaks with tongues, unless he interpret, that the assembly may receive edification" (v5). Tongues could be used for edification in the Assembly, but only if they were translated, and with a translated tongue it was the message that edified ***not*** the fact that it was in a foreign language. In fact, the tongue, in that it had to be translated, served to be a ***hindrance*** to the delivery of the message—hence the inferiority of tongues to prophecy in the Assembly. By contrast, outside the Assembly edification of believers was not in view at all and tongues served their primary purpose as a sign to unbelievers (the tongue, not the message as such, being the sign).

In verse 23 Paul says that "If therefore the whole assembly come together in one place, and all speak with tongues, and simple [persons] enter in, or unbelievers, will not they say ye are mad?" This is often taken to mean that Paul is criticising the tongue–speakers for speaking at the same time as each other, but this cannot be the sense since to be consistent the following verse would then have to be taken to mean that several prophets speaking at once is commendable (which contradicts verse 31 where the apostle shows the need to prophesy "one by one"). What he is saying is that if in an Assembly all speaking was only in tongues, this would be justly dismissed as madness by simple persons and unbelievers coming in. What kind of religion is it where no one understands each other? Imagine a visitor asking one of the Corinthian saints what was being said and being told that actually they didn't know! Such visitors would be most unlikely to say to the Corinthians "God is indeed amongst you" (see v25)! No, if tongue–speaking is to take place in the Assembly there ought at the very least to be room given for translation or, better still, the expression of the more appropriate gift—prophecy.

It must not be assumed that because the Corinthians spoke in tongues that ***every*** Assembly was so gifted. If we stick to the facts, we shall accept that Scripture does not mention tongues in connection with the vast majority of NT Assemblies. The Corinthian saints spoke in tongues because Corinth was a city containing a significant Jewish minority (see Acts 18: 7, 8), in view of which the gift was primarily distributed. Nor should we imagine that all the saints in Corinth could speak in tongues or were intended to in the ways of God. Many assert that not speaking in tongues implies a defect in one's faith, but 1 Cor. 12: 30, "do all speak with tongues?", is phrased in such a way as to demand a negative answer.

To sum up then, it can be seen that the real intention of the gift of tongues was as a sign to Israel of coming judgement. The gift might be used in a secondary way to deliver "the great things of God" (Acts 2: 11), or to edify the Assembly (see 1 Cor. 14: 5), but the primary purpose was as a sign (see 1 Cor. 14: 22). Matt. 16: 4 has been cited in a vain attempt to prove that tongues could not be a sign to the Jews specifically since the Lord said they would only be given the sign of Jonas. If we go to John 12: 37, however, we read that "though he had done so many signs before them, they believed not on him". Clearly, the Jews were given many signs. What the Lord meant in Matt. 16: 4 was a sign given in response to an unbelieving request to prove He was the Christ. The other signs were given without prompting. Having been unmoved by the witness that Jesus was the Christ, the nation would be sent a sign of impending judgement. The use of tongues (see Acts 2: 4) and Peter's urgent words "Be saved from this perverse generation" (v 40) go hand in hand. The Roman assault of AD70 (see Matt. 24: 2), brought about the fulfilment of what was foretold.

Now if the destruction of Jerusalem by Titus in AD70 brought about the fulfilment of what was foretold by tongues, is it sensible to expect tongues today? Hardly! Their purpose has been long since accomplished. Tongues were a divine warning to Israel of coming judgement if the Holy Spirit's testimony to an exalted Messiah was refused. That testimony was rejected, and the judgement fell, and with that tongues ceased to be needed—their purpose had run its course. It is futile to point to what many believe is a resurgence of tongues today. That something is happening in the modern church is undeniable. That it is ***not*** the same as what is presented in the Scriptures is, however, equally clear. The cry of the Reformers was *Sola Scriptura*—Scripture only. Sadly, Protestantism (so–called) appears to be abandoning that worthy motto. May you and I be found swimming against this tide!

Printed in Great Britain
by Amazon

25961621R00056